PREFACE.

People who are born in the beautiful Island of Guernsey are known as Guernsey Donkeys. The reason being, they can carry a very heavy load physically and mentally, they are willing to be lead, but refuse to be pushed, and they are very, very stubborn and are proud of it.

With all this in mind, at the end of the German occupation of our Island I painted on canvas what I thought was a fair indication of how we Islanders felt, and so am using it as the cover for my book. The painting was entitled "The Donkey did not Yield".

First published 2011 by Melody Press Printers
L'Islet, Guernsey, GY2 4SD

Designed, printed and bound by
Melody Press Printers

THIS BOOK IS DEDICATED TO MY PRECIOUS CHILDREN
WHO HAPPILY DID NOT HAVE TO LIVE THROUGH THE
OCCUPATION.

Deirdre, Gary, Mandy, Christopher and Sarah.

Also my darling grandchildren:

Stevie, Georgina, Eleanor, Natalie, Rebecca, Jacob, Remi, Louis,
Marley and Sammy, and my Sacha who is now safely in the
arms of Jesus.

Also my Great grandchildren:

Maddison and Shanice.

ACKNOWLEDGEMENTS.

Very many thanks to Stevie Regan and James Edmonds for their invaluable help each time I needed it with lap top problems.

Thanks too to Christopher Regan who not only did the reading but put my manuscript on a disc for me.

Also thanks to Barrie Smith for the loan of his occupation snapshots.

EXCUSE ME, I'M OCCUPIED.

By

PEARL WHITE-REGAN.

PEARL WHITE-REGAN
Beachcroft
La rue de la Saline,
Castel
Guernsey GY5 7XG.

EXCUSE ME, I'M OCCUPIED.

Chapter 1.

I was born in the Island of Guernsey in 1926. Life there was absolutely idyllic. People fell in love and when they married, it was "until death do us part". Whether times were good or bad they weathered the storms together. So different from today when as soon as a little bit of boredom sets in some men dump their wife and their children to set up home with some young floozy regardless of the sadness and loneliness they leave behind them.

No, things were different in the thirties when I was little, married couples stayed together, and children were safe and happy in the knowledge that in times of trouble, Mum and Dad were always there to turn to.

My parents adored each other, and my sister Gwen and I adored them. Gwen was eighteen months older than me but I soon caught her up height wise and as we looked so much alike, we were taken as twins and that pleased us and very soon we became known as the Smith twins.

When Gwen became school age we both began piano lessons. A lovely lady, Miss Mildred Bougourd, came to our house each Tuesday and Friday afternoon and began to teach us how to play. It soon became evident that Gwen was the gifted one, with me it was very heavy going. When it became time for us to take an exam, our teacher would arrive with the music we had to learn, and I would sit at the piano following first the notes for the right hand and working them out on the keyboard, then the left hand and so on until several days later after hours of work I could produce something like the finished piece should sound. Gwen on the other hand would settle down comfortably in an armchair surrounded by cushions with the music book lying open on her knees, and after an hour or so of study she would place the music book on the piano and begin to play!

We also took dancing lessons, Tap dancing, ballet, acrobatic and Greek. Our afternoons after school were pretty packed learning something or the other. I can remember taking violin lessons, my teacher was a small Scottish man known as Jock – well what else? And I did not enjoy these lessons one bit, perhaps it was because Gwen did not learn as well, I don't know. I used to end my prayers each night by asking for something to happen so I could give up the violin. Imagine my horror when mother sat beside me one day and taking both my hands in hers said she had something to tell me, and I must be very brave. Well, that made me shake with fright before she spoke again. There had been a car accident the night before in St. Julians Avenue, Jock was in the car and he had been killed. I was mortified, my prayer had been answered, but I had not wanted him to die. It was many years before the weight of guilt lifted from my shoulders but I never took my violin out of its case again.

On one dreadful day our dancing teacher, Billy Regan, was taking us back to school after we had been to his house for lunch, and we squeezed into the front of his car. I was in the middle and was so squashed I could scarcely breathe, then as we turned the corner into Les Rocquettes lane which led to our school, suddenly I had more room, and pushing up towards Gwen I realized she was not there and the door was wide open. I yelled, and Billy Regan jammed on the brakes. We found her lying on the road and her left arm was very badly injured around the wrist and elbow. Fortunately no bones were broken and the very next day we had a piano examination. She flatly refused to not sit the exam, so with her left arm bandaged from wrist to elbow and an explanation from our teacher, she sat the exam. She passed it , but that was the only exam she ever passed without distinction!

We had two St. Bernard dogs, Rupert and Cedric, and apart from my sister they were my very best friends. I was cycling up the lane outside our house one beautiful summer morning, dressed only in my bathing suit, and Rupert was ambling along beside me. When we got to the top of the lane, I cycled around ready to cycle back to home, but somehow something went wrong with the way I was steering and I hit the bank and landed up in a hedge full of stinging nettles. I remember lying there in terrible agony, then I felt teeth grabbing hold of the straps of my bathing suit, and pulling me free from the nettles. Then I was dragged back down back the lane and deposited by the back door of our house, and I heard the whining and crying of Rupert until my mother opened the door to find out what was happening. By then the nettle stings were clearly visible and even more clearly felt as she helped me up and took me inside! Rupert had indeed proved that he was a rescue dog!

Several weeks later on a Sunday afternoon, we were dressed in our best Sunday clothes and intended to visit my Father's family who lived in Hauteville. I was ready first, and resplendent in a gorgeous frock of Ruby coloured velvet, with new white socks and patent shoes, I was allowed outside to wait for everybody else on the strict understanding I would get up to no mischief-as if I would. I walked quietly round to the back garden and came face to face with the six foot fence and gate built purposely to keep our lovely dogs from wandering. They were both with me at the time, and although I wanted to pass and walk through the fields on the other side. I knew very well that if I opened the gate the two dogs would rush past me and escape. There was only one thing for it. Holding my skirt up out of the way I started to climb the fence. I got to the top quite easily and standing on the top rail I got ready to jump. It seemed a long way down, but jumping was the only solution to getting down on the other side.

Throwing caution to the wind I leapt, but unfortunately my skirt was caught over one of the upright stakes and I found myself hanging, arms and legs dangling, half way between the top of the fence and the ground. I do not know how long I would have hung there, but I suddenly heard the faint sound of material ripping and with fear in my heart I knew my lovely new dress had had it. Rip, rip, and then one enormous tear and I landed on the ground with a bump. I leave the rest of what happened after that to the imagination of the reader.

My parents had an agreement with several of the colleges in Oxford that when any students living too far away from home had holidays, they would come and study at Les Pieux. We set a room aside for them with a very large table in it and there they were able to study undisturbed. Nothing was ever moved, it was THEIR room and theirs alone.

They were lovely gentlemen, one in particular came from South Africa, and with a lot of patience, he eventually taught me a song in South African, and although that was eighty odd years ago I can remember it to this day.

It was about this time that war clouds were hanging over Europe. It was in the month of September that two of the Oxford boys came in to our kitchen to hear the news on the radio with our parents, and while we all listened in absolute silence came the terrible words that no one wanted to hear.......

"We are now at war with Germany".

So the idyllic years of my childhood suddenly shattered like a broken mirror. I did not matter too much to us living on a little Island, nothing could change for us, but the poor Oxford boys, this was the end of their studies, and into the Services they would have to go.

Watching them pack up their belongings and leaving the Island was traumatic, but as all the adults agreed, it would only be a short while, perhaps until Christmas, then it would all be over.

We watched them get into a taxi the following day and my sister and I were both crying. Away they went to fight their war, and we all settled back to wait for the dreadful war to finish so that life could carry on as before.

Only, it did not work out quite like that.

Finally Christmas came around, but there was no sign of the war ending, in fact things were getting worse with each day. Hitler sent his troops all over Europe, fighting and claiming countries that did not belong to him and we waited and waited impatiently for it all to end.

The optimism among the Guernsey people soon turned to pessimism as weeks turned into months and we all began to realize we were in for a long winter.

It was just after my thirteenth birthday and I was going through that terrible stage of leaving childhood behind and coping with being an adult, terrible time, when I wanted to appear grown up in front of my family, but welcomed bedtime when I could nurse my doll and tell her all my troubles.

Gwen and I carried on with our dancing and piano lessons, and I also started taking singing lessons which I loved, we used to sit at the piano and spend hours just singing in harmony and entertaining our family and friends.

We performed in various concerts, and finally in the local Eisteddfod and were very fortunate to walk away with prizes.

Our dancing teacher entered us in a competition held at the Royal Hotel, and we did a duet called "Everything Stops for Tea". We won first prize for our class, and as a result had to go to London to dance in a concert at Conway Hall in aid of Dr Barnardos Home for Blind Babies.

What excitement, an early arrival at the harbour where we met other dancers lucky enough to have won, and on to the steamer we all trooped ready for the great adventure. I had never sailed on a large boat before, but it was then that I discovered that I was not a good sailor.

The journey seemed to last for ever, I have never been so ill but at last, we were walking down the gangway and it was over. Then the train ride into London. That was something else. Passing fields with black and white cattle, so different to our brown and cream cows at home, and then through picturesque small villages, and finally London. All the bright lights, noise and bustle, then after the train, the ride in the taxi to our hotel in more traffic than I could have imagined in my wildest dreams.

After breakfast we all went to Conway Hall to rehearse for the evenings performance. My goodness! A bit different to the halls we were used to performing in at home, and the spectators' area was enormous, quite intimidating in fact, but once we were dressed in our costumes and the band struck up our music, everything fell into place, and by the evening all went without a hitch and the whole concert was a huge success.

Life seemed very tame when we went back home, I had had a taste of what was going on outside of our Island and I had a sudden desire to see more of the world. What a miserable time to get this desire. Time passed slowly by, and the awful war took its toll.

Then came the awful news that the Island's population was to be evacuated. It was not compulsory, but every family had to decide either to go together, or the children could go with the school they were attending. Well, it was definitely decided by my parents that no way would we be parted and if we did evacuate we would all go together as a family. It was several days of indecision, posters appeared all over the Island saying there was no place like home, and don't be yellow don't go away. What a decision for parents to have to make. Hundreds of small school children kissed their parents a tearful goodbye and set off to live among complete strangers for what turned out to be many years.

My parents toyed with the idea of going, but I do not think they ever really considered it a pliable option. Many families packed small suitcases and walked out of their front doors leaving their family pets, cats, dogs and many other animals behind to fend for themselves or perish in the attempt!

For a few days everything was in an uproar and we settled back down to get our breath back and muse over whether we had made the right decision or not, we did not have to wait long to find out, and by then it was too late!

Chapter 2.

I sat in the bay window of one of the lounges in my parent's hotel and looked out on to beautiful Cobo Bay. The liquid turquoise of the sea spread its silver lace edging over the golden sand and as I surveyed the lovely scene before me I felt that all was well with my world.

My sister had gone up the road to the corner shop to buy sweets for us to share that evening as we sat and listened to the radio. The rumbling I could hear in the distance sounded like thunder but I knew on such a lovely day what it really was- the huge heavy guns on the coast of France spitting out their venom at the enemies on their shores.

I breathed a sigh of relief that we lived on an Island, no way could the sound of Jackboots echo through our streets as they had in the various countries in Europe, we were safe thanks to the seas that surrounded our shores.

I leaned forward to see up the road whether my sister was on her way, and at that moment she rounded the corner and was in full view carrying two bags of sweets in her hands.

It was at the very moment I saw my sister Gwen, that I heard it. An aeroplane coming in very low, followed by a sound which I had never heard before, but I instinctively knew was machine gunning. I saw chips of granite flying up into the air from the wall on the opposite side of the road on which Gwen was now running.

Out of the corner of my eye I saw my father sprinting down the drive and into the road where he swept my sister into his arms and raced for the house. I met them in the hall where my mother was already waiting and we grabbed each other and huddled together, crying in relief.

The floor seemed to be vibrating and we could hear muffled explosions in the distance and although we did not know it at the time a dreadful air raid was being held on the harbour in St. Peter Port where many local growers had their baskets of tomatoes in lorries queued up waiting for transport to England. Many of the drivers threw themselves under their lorry in an attempt to save their lives only to lose it as the German 'planes flew low and bombed heavily. In weeks ahead, the Germans maintained that their pilots thought the lorries contained military personnel waiting to be shipped to the Mainland.

Anyway here we were on June 29th 1940 huddled together in the hallway of our home unaware of what the future held, just grateful that my Gwen was safe after her frightful ordeal, and quite confident that all the trauma was over and done with, but if only we had known it had only just begun.

The following day, I heard a word that I was unfamiliar with, rumour, and it was to become a word used and heard for many years to come.

It became rumoured the following day that the Germans had landed, but we could not believe this to be true.

In the meantime we received a telephone call from my paternal grandmother who lived in the heart of St. Peter Port to say that all her windows had been blown out during the air raid and could she come with my aunt to stay with us. Of course we readily agreed, but there was something else, could her neighbours come too as their son had been in the bath at the time of the raid. When the first bomb dropped, the whole house and especially the bath, shuddered and sent the bath water splashing over the sides. Their son made a desperate effort to stand up but a second bomb dropped and he fell back into the bath with an almighty splash. It was then that the third bomb landed and the window was blown in covering him with a shower of broken glass. As he stared in disbelief at the mess he was in, another explosion blew a dead seagull through the broken window and it landed with an almighty bang on his bare chest.

Because of the war we had no guests at the hotel at the time so we readily agreed and welcomed them in.

My grandmother was a very religious lady and spent quite a lot of her time reading her bible, and this was what she was doing at the dining room table when my aunt walked in a tray full of dishes which were clean and ready to be put away. As she entered the room her sleeve caught on the handle of the door and the tray was swept from her hands and landed with one almighty crash behind my Grandma's chair.

The shock was so great after the trauma of the last day that she leapt from her chair and came out with such profane language that none of us thought she even knew, she then retired to her room and spent an hour or so begging God for forgiveness.

After that things settled down until the next morning when a bus load of German officers drove in and parked in our driveway. My father went out to meet them and of course my mother, sister and I followed in his wake.

The German held his hand out, but when my father ignored it he let it drop to his side.

"I understand you are living alone here with your family" he said in perfect English.

"No, I have my mother and sister here together with their next door neighbours as they have been bombed out".

"I am sorry to hear that, but that is how things happen in wartime, however they must vacate their rooms with immediate effect as I need these rooms for my officers" and the tone of his voice left no room for argument.

"I will see the rooms now and tell you which ones I require and which ones you can keep", and with this he walked past my father and made for the front door.

"Now just a minute-" began my father but my mother grabbed his arm and shook her head and he followed the German into the hotel.

My parents were given a bedroom and my sister and I were to share another. We had sole use of the kitchen and could use the dining room and lounge if they were not in use by the officers living in the house.

He then went outside and giving an order in a loud authorative voice demanded the soldiers in the bus to get out and stand around in the garden. I particularly remember the strong smell of leather from their boots and the overpowering smell of eau de cologne, a smell which was to become very familiar during the occupation as the occupying forces seemed to wash in it whether water was available or not.

I think this is a very good time to introduce Sister Young. She came over to Guernsey about a year before the occupation and was welcomed into a private nursing home here as a senior nurse. She came from Ireland and her strong Irish brogue gave that away. She was very pretty with jet black hair and the bluest eyes I had ever seen.

We met her when my sister was admitted to the nursing home as a private patient when she had to have her tonsils removed, and Sister Young was asked to nurse her. She was very kind to Gwen and extremely helpful and a great comfort to us all when we visited. It resulted in her being invited to tea on the first Sunday that Gwen returned home and she became such a friend that whenever she was not on duty she would spend every moment of her spare time with us.

I clearly remember her opening words when ever she arrived on our door step, in a strong Irish accent she would always say;-

"Well what's been happening, anythin' strange or startling, wha' ?"

She was so sweet and we all loved her.

The amazing thing was that from the moment the Germans invaded she simply disappeared from the scene and we did not hear from her for many, many months, and then it was under the most bizarre circumstances, but that will come later in this story!

Our guests from St. Peter Port were taken back to their windowless homes and our home was invaded in the true sense of the word by the occupying troops.

Life as a child, I was only 13 at the time, and having grown up in a hotel I was quite used to meeting strangers on the stairs or in the halls although not dressed in those uniforms or greeting me in that language. Things were much as usual until the first local Press was delivered on July 1st. and contained orders for the residents of Guernsey as given by the Commandant of the Island and read as follows;-

All inhabitants must be indoors by 11p.m. and not leave before 6a.m.

We all respect population of Guernsey but should anyone attempt to cause the least trouble serious measures will be taken and the town blown up (bombed).

All orders given by Military Authorities are to be strictly obeyed.

All spirits must be locked up immediately and no spirits may be supplied henceforth. This prohibition does not apply to private homes.

No person shall enter into the Aerodrome at La Villiaze.

All rifles, air guns, pistols, revolvers, sporting guns and all other weapons except souvenirs must together with ammunition be delivered at Royal Hotel by 12 o'clock today July 1st.

All British Sailors, Airmen and Soldiers on leave in this Island must report at the Police Station at 9 a.m. today and must then report to the Royal Hotel.

No boats or vessels of any description including any fishing boats shall leave the harbour or any other place where same is moored without an order from Military Authorities. All boats arriving from Jersey, Sark or Herm or elsewhere must remain in the harbour until permitted by the Military to leave. The crew will remain on board and the master will report to the harbour master St Peter Port and will obey his instructions.

The sale of motor spirits is prohibited except for the use of essential services such as Doctors, vehicles delivering food stuffs, sanitary services, and any vehicle in possession of a permit from the Military authorities.

The blackout regulations already in force must be observed as before.

Banks and shops will be open as usual.

Signed by the German Commandant of the Island of Guernsey.

The first day was a nightmare on the roads because we were still driving and riding on the left, and they were careering around on the right side, but this soon came to an end when a law was made by the occupying forces that all vehicles using the road must drive on the right which meant more confusion for us.

Then on July 10th, the notice in the Guernsey Press that the rationing of various essential commodities had tightened again. Meat, bacon, clothes, sugar, beer, and candles. There would be two meatless days a week and meat could be purchased up to 1/- per head per week. Bacon was to be strictly rationed as was sugar.

Bacon, cooked and boneless	3 ozs per person.
Bacon, uncooked with bone	4 ozs
Butter	4 ozs
Sugar	6 ozs.

Sale of candles prohibited.

Then to save on gas and electricity both services would be turned off from the main at 9 o'clock each evening and turned on again at 6 in the morning. Like all the other new differences in our life this took a lot of getting used to.

I remember one evening my mother was cooking sugar beet and had almost finished when the gas popped off. She was absolutely furious, and with a hugh puff of anger she pushed the saucepan to the back of the stove and left the kitchen.

My father, always an early riser was first in the kitchen and was greeted by a strong smell of gas. Guessing what had happened he rushed in, turned off the tap that my mother had failed to do the night before, opened the windows and it was then he discovered our two little canaries lying in the bottom of their cage with their legs in the air, they had been gassed. Fortunately my lovely German Shepherd dog, Risky, slept in my bedroom and I dread to think what might have been her fate had she slept in the kitchen.

Our hotel comprised of two buildings and it was my parents intention to join them up by a ballroom with bedrooms on top which each would have commanded a beautiful view of Cobo Bay, this of course was all pie in the sky for after the war because as we all knew it would all be over by Christmas, only nobody said 'which' Christmas. At that time however, that part of the hotel was unoccupied until the Germans commandeered it and filled it with foreign workers which they brought over from Europe as forced labour. These poor people were just skin and bone which was easy to see as their clothes were falling off them and most of them had sacking on their feet as a make-shift for shoes.

Each evening when they got back from their labours, a lorry would drive up with two dustbins in the back filled with what looked like cabbage water, and the driver would shout;

"A la soup"

Then out would shuffle the poor souls with old tins or bits of broken soup dishes to get a ladle full, then would gulp it down to be able to queue up again in the hope of a second helping. So often after rushing their first portion they would find they were too late and the bins were empty.

We used to feel so sorry for them being so far away from home and so very hungry, we had no idea at that time what the future held for us, that there would come a time when we would have empty cupboards and no earthly way of filling them. Still, our consolation was that we were all together as a family, so many of our friends had had their family torn apart by allowing some of their children to evacuate with their schools, little knowing it would be five long years before they saw each other again. One friend of mine evacuated with her school at the tender age of five, leaving behind her parents and baby sister. On her return five years later her mother was going through her daughter's schoolbooks and she found a letter written by her little girl when she first arrived in England and this is what she wrote:

"Darling Mummy,

I do not like it here, I have not got any money, I am very unhappy and want to come home. Please will you come and get me.

It must have almost broken that mother's heart to read that, but decisions had to be made very quickly and the pamphlets stuck up all over the Island did not help, saying:

"Stay at home, don't be yellow" and

"There's no place like home" but when your children's lives' were in danger which way was the safest?

So the trauma began, the first of very many decisions the inhabitants of Guernsey would have to make, but then it would only be until Christmas!!!

I wrote a lot of poetry during the war and I am including one every now and again

Evacuation
Poem wrote circa 1940

At evacuation time they gave out leaflets

"Don't be yellow," "Stay at Home," and such clap trap;

The German Reich won't bother with these Islands

Guernsey's just a full stop on the map.

"Don't abandon your homes in sudden panic,

Don't part from those you love in sudden flight";

So we stayed the next step? The invasion –

And Guernsey is just a full stop now, all right!

We find this situation is confusing,

No one knows where they are going, quite,

Especially when it comes to transportation

We're on the left – the Germans on the right!

The States officials warn us "Don't be hasty",

To be a martyr now is not your lot;

There's nowhere you can run if you're discovered

And it's ten to one your family will be shot.

So we keep the rules, and never break the curfew,

And go our different ways with tongue in cheek,

We have promised that we will not cause reprisals;

But it's difficult as week replaces week.

Now, I'm very good at minding my own business,

And I'm above an act of sabotage by far;

So I don't know where that English soldier's hiding

And I've no idea who stole that German's car !!

Chapter 3.

As the days turned into weeks, and the weeks into months, I became so accustomed to the men living in our house that I almost forgot they were the enemy. If I had had a father or a brother away fighting for his country my outlook would have no doubt been very different, but as things were they were very polite young men who spoke very good English, but as it turned out the fore runners of the occupying forces had been hand picked which became evident as time wore on, gradually their manner, their speech and eventually their brutality changed with each new batch of soldiers that were sent to occupy us.

The original men that stayed in our home were well mannered, easy to talk to, and loved to show us photographs of their families and I felt no fear in their company at all. What I did fear and abhorred was the frightful "tarty" women they invited to their parties.

I remember one night in particular I was crossing the hall when all of a sudden the lounge door flew open and a stout elderly woman very highly and badly made up brushed past me sending me falling against the wall. I can still remember the strong odour of her, a mixture of cheap perfume and alcohol.

"Out of my way, child" she hissed and made a bee-line for the stairs.

I stood for ages waiting for her to come down so that I could climb the stairs to bed. At last she turned the bend of the stairs and came into view. She swayed uncertainly down and finally landed with a plop on the last stair. She just sat there staring into space. I was not sure if I had the courage to pass her, but if I was to get to my room there was nothing for it.

Standing in front of her I said

"Will you excuse me please, I wish to go upstairs"

"Help yourself dear" she replied but made no effort to move.

To pass her would have meant stepping on her dress which was spread across the stair on either side of her. I bent forward to lift the dress a little so I could put my foot down but she slapped my wrist and said

"Don't do that, have you any idea how much this dress cost"? I rushed past her and up the stairs, expecting any minute to feel her greasy hot hand grab my ankle and pull me down to the bottom again but I made it to the top and straightening up I dared to look down at her and she was sitting there with two fists up to her eyes as if holding a pair of binoculars and she was muttering,

"I see no ships, only ruddy hardships" and as she burst into stupid laughter, I turned the bend in the stairs and ran up to my room carefully locking the door behind me as I entered. I do not remember ever seeing her again.

When reading or just sitting quietly, I had a habit of twisting my ring around my finger. It was a signet ring which my parents had given me on my birthday and it had my initials P.S. engraved on it. To my horror it was not on my finger. I sat a few minutes trying to remember when last I had had it. Then I remembered. I had taken it off in the bathroom after lunch to wash my hands. With a sigh of relief I got up and made for the stairs. Once in the bathroom I went straight to the basin but there was only an empty space where I knew I had left it. I searched everywhere, all around the floor, the window sill, everywhere, but no ring was to be found it had apparently vanished into thin air!!

Several days later a young Guernsey girl called to see her German boy friend and I met her in the hall way as she arrived. While we were chatting I suddenly noticed she was wearing my ring. Being young and gauche I did not have the courage to ask her outright but went a little out of my way to say to her,

"That is a lovely ring you are wearing"

Yes, "she replied, "it is my engagement ring, Peter and I are to be married after the war"

"Are those your initials" I asked in what I hoped she thought was all innocence.

"Oh no" she laughed "Peter had those engraved on himself they stand for Peter and Suzy"

Oh no they don't I thought to myself, they stand for Pearl Smith, and hurried off to the kitchen to find my mother. I reached her and tried to tell her the whole story amidst a floor of tears, and begged her to go to the girl and get me my ring back.

My mother sat down and took both my hands in hers.

"Pearly love," she said, " we are living in very troubled times, and there is no way I can risk calling a German a thief, or a liar, people have been shot for less than that. Anyway, you are growing so fast that old ring would not have fitted you for long, so as soon as this wicked war is over, your father and I will buy you a bigger and better one, and that is a promise. Now, dry your eyes and forget about the stupid girl and her hopes of a wedding after the war."

I did not forget, and no one but me knew that I hated Peter more than any other German in the world.

One miserable windy and rainy day I was walking up the hall with my mother, and the lounge door was open, and we saw a German officer standing on one of the dining-room chairs singing to an appreciative audience of his colleagues.

My mother who was very house-proud by nature flew into the room and knocked the stupid fellow off the chair.

"How dare you stand on my good chairs with your filthy muddy boots, I wouldn't allow my children to stand on our chairs with their shoes on".

He got unsteadily to his feet, and it became apparent that he was drunk.

He went up so close to mum, that his nose was almost touching hers. She drew swiftly back towards me.

"How dare you, a filthy English woman, speak to a German Officer in that tone, and to dare to push me off the chair, there is only one way to teach you a lesson, I am going to have to shoot you".

His fellow officers dashed to their feet to restrain him. I was petrified and flew outside to the wing-end of the house where the Commandant of Alderney was resting for a few days.

I hammered on the door and he opened it almost at once and listened to my hysterical outburst. He passed me and made for the main house. I ran swiftly behind him and on entering the hall he grabbed his belt off the hall stand and made for the outside door murmuring as he went

"If he is going to shoot her, he won't do it with my gun" and disappeared from sight.

However, the drunkard had been pacified with more alcohol by now, and my mother was safely ensconced in the kitchen.

Ulrich Dreier was a young Leutnant known to his friends as Oolie. He was one of the unluckiest human beings it had ever been my misfortune to meet.

His face bore two deep scars from two separate skiing accidents, and his slight limp was the result of a previous spill on his motor bike when he sustained various injuries including a broken leg.

I once saw him sitting with a cup and saucer filled with piping hot tea resting on his knee. A senior officer entered the room, and Oolie jumped to his feet to salute, and in so doing broke both the cup and saucer, as well as scalding his leg with the tea.

He appeared at our house one evening having been invited by the officers billeted with us on the occasion of his birthday. He had miraculously reached the age of twenty-one. A man at last!

All the maternal instincts in my mother came to the fore; she wanted to do some little thing to make the day memorable for him. Smiling sweetly at my father she suggested;

"How about if I take him in the carrot cake I made toda-"

"No way" interrupted my father, "give food to a German when we are so short, no way"

"But just imagine if we had a son and he was celebrating his twenty-first birthday miles away from home, we would be glad if someone took him under their wing "

"Well we haven't got a son, only two daughters who need every crumb we can give them"

"But I can get more carrots where I got these from and-"

My father cut her short, and as always whenever they had a disagreement Dad gave in. "Please yourself, do what you want to do" and he kissed her.

She put the precious cake on a plate, and rummaging around in a kitchen drawer came up with a birthday cake candle. It had obviously been used before, the wick was black, but she pushed it into the cake and before we marched in to the lounge she lit it.

The moment we entered the room all chattering stopped, and my mother stepped forward and handed the cake to Oolie and wished him all the best for the future.

He took the plate from her with trembling hands and I feared he was going to cry, but instead with a lovely smile he said;

"I am very touched that an English lady with a family to feed has given food to a German, you will never know how much I appreciate this" and shaking her hand continued "for as long as I live I will never forget your kindness".

The party continued well into the night, and eventually the birthday boy celebrated to such an extent that one of the other officers had to take him home and he left his car at our house. The next day he was given a lift by a fellow officer to come to us to retrieve his car. It was a dreadful day weather-wise, pouring with rain and dark thunder clouds overhead, and they skidded and had a fatal accident, the last one poor Oolie would ever have.

When the news of his death reached us, his final words echoed in my head.

"For as long as I live, I will never forget your kindness.......For as long as I live......."

Invasion

Poem wrote circa 1942

The Germans have invaded lovely Guernsey

Their Jackboots tramp on road, and soul and mind,

And as the months stretch hopelessly to sad years

Nourishment and hope are hard to find.

I miss the part of growing up the sane way,

I miss the piece of life I can't get back,

I miss the lovely open road of freemen;

I'm tired of this scary one way track.

I miss the luxuries we took for granted,

Especially the one the world calls food;

And all the lovely words called hope and beauty,

They've been replaced with words like lean and crude!

I'll be glad when this occupations over

I'll be glad to see the ugly jackboots flee,

But the sad thing is if I get any hungrier,

When the end comes, will I still be here to see?

Chapter 4.

It was at just about this time that the worst rumour yet began to circulate in the community. We were told that any man who had not been born in Guernsey together with his family was to be sent to a prison camp in Germany. We were horrified as my father was born in Scotland.

"Lets not panic" my father tried to pacify us "it may be a lot of rubbish, let us wait and see what happens in the next few days and not meet trouble half way".

Several days passed and we began to think that Dad was right, then as we settled for a meal late one afternoon we heard the dreaded sound of a motor bike pulling into the drive followed by the crunch of jack boots on the gravel outside the kitchen window, and then the pounding on the back door.

"Oh no!" groaned my mother. Dad squeezed her shoulder as he made to answer the door.

We waited with bated breath and when he returned his face said it all.

We were to be sent away with hardly any time to spare to prepare ourselves and were to assemble at St. Matthews church the following Thursday taking with us only enough clothes to fill a suitcase that we could comfortably carry.

The next few days were hectic. Mother had set up emergency supplies in what she called her store cupboard. There were dozens of tins of food stuff that she had purchased before rationing began. Realising that we would no longer be there to eat it after all, she filled some trucks from the greenhouses and with Gwen and I to help her, wheeled everything around to her mother's house to tell her the news and leave her the food. What a terrible time, we all kissed and hugged and cried, I was convinced I would never see my grandmother again.

Father, in the meantime, was very busy too. He had for several months been building rabbit hutches, and filling them with rabbits with the intention of breeding as food for us all in the future. Now it seemed there was to be no future here for us so he went among his friends and gave away all the hutches complete with rabbits.

Mum returned home and covered all her most precious furniture with dust sheets, I wondered at the time how long those sheets would remain in place once we shut the front door for good. Gwen and I with our mother's help packed what we thought necessary in the way of clothes, and finally the dreaded day arrived.

Our family walked down the road for a final farewell to Mum's family and we returned home to wait for the moment to come when we would have to make the dreadful walk up to the church.

As we waited in silence for the moment to arrive we were all startled by the telephone ringing. My father was gone for quite a few minutes to answer it and when he returned he had a most puzzled expression on his face.

"What is it?" my mother hardly dared to ask," what is the matter, what's wrong?"

In a very puzzled voice he replied

"That was Sister Young, she says I must report to the Commandant's office in the Grange at once."

"Sister Young? Did you tell her that we have to be at the Church in half an hour, you won't have time to go there?"

"Yes, I told her all that and she said it was an order from the Commandant himself and I was to go at once".

As we watched him go, my mother was in tears again.

"We are going to be in so much trouble, what will happen if he is not back in time do we go on without him?"

We all agreed that would be a terrible mistake and we should just stay put and see what happened.

It was almost two hours later before he returned and mum was beside herself and almost choking with fear.

"We have missed the deadline," she sobbed "what will happen to us now?"

My father took her gently in his arms and kissed her.

"Our worries are over for the present, we don't have to go today."

"Why, what has happened, tell me for goodness sake"

"Well- I was met at the door by Sister Young, it seems she works there and also, she speaks German like a native."

"So yes, go on"

"Well she took me into the Commandants office and explained who I was. He was very polite and said that Sister Young had told him about our situation and he said that although no meat was getting through at the present he hoped we would soon be able to get supplies through from France. In this event, he continued we will need your services to distribute rations so I must insist that you remain on the Island for that purpose. You and your family are exempt from leaving the Island today, but this is only temporary. However, he continued, you will need to be occupied, so I want you to present yourself at Rockmount Hotel in the morning and there you will expected to help prepare food for the forced labour on the Island."

My mother could only stare with her mouth wide open.

"I don't believe it" she gasped "you mean we don't have to go after all?"

"That's right "laughed dad.

"But what about all my food I gave away and our rabbits?"

"I think it was well worth the sacrifice don't you, now get your coats off and lets get back to normal" dad took his coat off and threw it over the back of the nearest chair.

"Back to normal" scoffed Mum, "will we ever be in that happy state again?"

My half sister gave Gwen the clothes and jewellery back that she had given her the day before, but my cousin refused to return mine saying that a gift for a day was a gift for ever!"

We took all the dust sheets off and everyone was in a jolly mood, we had been spared the most horrific ordeal and it was all thanks to Sister Young. It was then that doubts began to spring into our minds. Who exactly was she? and how come she spoke such perfect German and why was she working for the Commandant of the Island, and how come her words had brought such pressure to bear. Suddenly the idea formed into my parent's minds. Could she have been a fifth columnist sent here in advance to pave the way for the invasion? It seemed quite feasible but we would never know for sure!

My mothers' brother however, was not as lucky as we were, although a Guernsey man born and bred, it became his destiny to be sent to a prison camp known as Laufen, and here is the reason why.

Just before hostilities began, a pretty Jewish girl fled to Guernsey with a close friend to escape as the German forces closed in across Europe, her choice of the Island was unfortunate, had she gone a little further afield into England her story would have been very different. However she and her friend Auguste Spitz chose Guernsey where the pretty Jewish girl, Elisabet Fink, found work as an au pair for a local family.

In the course of her duties she quite often had to visit the Cobo Post Office where my uncle Harry served as the Post Master, and this is how they met. I remember my uncle telling my mother about her. Now, he had been a widower for several years, and as he neither womanized, or went out clubbing, and although he was very lonely after the death of his wife, his hopes of finding another partner were very slim.

Then suddenly this pretty foreign girl showed him attention, he explained to my mother that as he lived alone he was worried how to advance this friendship. My mother suggested that he come to tea the next Sunday and ask her if she would like to accompany him.

She was delighted and the afternoon was a tremendous success. My sister and I played the piano and afterwards Elisabet sat down and played and sang to us.

I remember the very first tune I ever heard her play, it was "One day when we were young" and she had a lovely singing voice. My uncle was sitting by the piano in a large armchair, and as she finished playing, she ran her thumb in a crescendo along the keyboard and followed it with her body, and let herself fall from the piano stool right on to my uncle's lap. We were delighted, and that was the start of a lovely romance. A few months before war broke out they were married in a little church in the north of the Island on February 12th, 1940, and everything looked 'rosey' but their happiness was short-lived when the Germans invaded Guernsey and began searching the Island for Jews.

Eventually a baby girl was born to complete their happiness, and they called her Janet. She was beautiful, and the apple of her father's eye. She was very intelligent too, and at an age when most toddlers were struggling to gasp the English language, she could sing the French national anthem from beginning to end, and in French!

However, their happiness was short lived, as all Jews in the Island had to register, and Elisabet had much longer curfew than the rest of us, and had a large badge with a capital "J" on which she was supposed to sew on to her outer clothing, but she never did.

Eventually they were sent to concentration camps, and the morning that they left brought more sorrow to my Grandmother who had already said goodbye to us when we thought we were going; and as Harry and Elisabet were leaving, little Janet, quite oblivious of the drama going on around her began to sing in her baby voice;

"Oh! Oh! Antonio

He's gone away," and as she disappeared from sight her little voice could still be heard---

"Left me alone-io

All on my own-io"

Then the tears fell like rain!

When we first moved into Les Pieux, Gwen and I were allowed to choose which room we wanted to have as our own. I chose a little room at the top of the first flight of stairs. There was another small room on the next landing and it had obviously been turned into a linen cupboard, as you entered there was a glass door in front of you which led out on to the front balcony. On your right was a dividing wall, and on your left large wooden doors which reached from the entrance door to the balcony door and were divided into two and could be opened in a sliding movement to reveal many shelves which had obviously been used to store linen. It was completely empty. Way above these shelves was another cupboard which I could only touch by standing on tip toe, this too appeared to be empty.

Gwen asked if she could have this as her room, and father said if the sliding doors and shelves were removed a single bed would fit in there quite easily, Gwen was delighted, and several days later the lower cupboards were gone, new linoleum laid, and a single bed erected into the empty space left by the removed cupboards, the top cupboards still remained but were no obstacle as they were near the ceiling.

Gwen could hardly wait to move in and the morning following we could hardly wait to ask her how her first night in her new room had been.

"Not good," she replied," it was fine at first, I fell asleep almost at once and not long afterwards I awoke and there was the most awful smell and as it got stronger and stronger as the night wore on and I could not get back to sleep, I am completely shattered".

The same thing happened for the next two nights and my parents were completely baffled. My mother suggested that perhaps a rat had crawled up and died in the top cupboard.

"How on earth could a rat get up there?" queried my father.

"Well they can get into lofts and cellars can't they".

"Alright I'll get my step ladder and have a good look in the top", replied my father going out to the shed to get his ladder.

Inquisitive as always, I followed him up the stairs to my sister's room. He climbed the ladder and slid the first door open. Peering into the gloom he assured me that there was nothing there, but as his eyes became accustomed to the light he said;

"Wait a minute, I can see something in the far corner". He climbed down from his ladder, and moving it forward went up again.

Sliding open the second door he reached well forward and pulled forward a rather large shopping bag with a zipped top.

Coming down to my level he smiled:

"Well I have found something, but it certainly does not smell".

We carried the bag downstairs and we all stood round eager for Dad to open the zip.

What a disappointment when all we found was a rolled up beach towel covered with what looked like rust stains.

Dad took the bag outside and left it by the dust bins, "The dustbin men can have that " he said "But we still don't know what caused the smell".

Later that afternoon two young Germans were passing and saw the bag. They saw my father in the shed and asked if the bag was rubbish and could they have it. My father said they could but would they just put the towels in the dust bin.

However the curiosity of the German mind prompted the young soldier to try to unwrap the towel but it was almost impossible as the rust stains held it firm. They tried between them but all to no avail, and so my father seeing they were determined to unwrap the bundle went indoors and brought out a poker with a claw at the end, used for riddling the ashes from the boiler, and gave it to them. By now we as a family were all curious to be in at the end of the mystery and stood around watching them.

Little by little they pulled off bits of the towel, until one rather large bit came away.

"Stop!" roared my father, "Hold it a minute" and walking closer said" Heavens above it's a little monkey", then picking up the bundle and looking closer exclaimed "Dear God, it's a human baby, I'm going to phone the police". With this he disappeared through the back door. When he returned we stood around everyone giving our opinion about what we thought could had happened to the wee mite.

Finally the police arrived and after asking a few preliminary questions put the little body back into the bag and took it away. Many enquiries were made by the police but all met with a dead end. Because of the war they could not extend their enquiries further afield. The case came to court and my father was asked to attend, which he did. It came to light that the rust stains were blood, and the body was that of a new born baby.

Because of the lack of evidence the case remained open, and the court adjourned.

Needless to say, Gwen never slept in that room again, but many guests did, and we never had a repeat of the complaint of an unnatural and unearthly smell.

No Escape
Poem wrote circa 1943

Some friends and I developed an escape plan,

To flee to England, there to do our bit,

But when we reached the place of embarkation,

Wide open mouthed, we nearly threw a fit!

We had posted off our notes of explanation

Of how we hoped to save the Motherland,

Then with "borrowed" food and Brandy in our knapsacks

We arrived to find our boat high on the sand.

No one had thought of checking the tide table,

We couldn't push the boat out in full view;

So daunted, we returned to face the music,

There was nothing else we could do!

We decided to repeat the whole maneuver,

Planning details carefully for days,

But before we finalized the day of the sailing

The German soldiers mined the Island's bays.

So now we're really trapped, there's no escaping,

We've got no choice, we're here and here to stay;

So back we sit and wait with nervous patience;

For that great moment – LIBERATION DAY!!!

Chapter 5.

My sister, Gwen and I had started to take dancing lessons when I was only two years old, and piano lessons a year later, so appearing in public was second nature to us. Every year we took part in the local Eisteddfod, many cabarets, various examinations in piano playing, and of course pantomimes at Christmas; so it was really no surprise when we were both invited to join the "Lyric No. 1" company. It was a theatrical company that performed regularly to entertain the public and to put a little fun and laughter into the hum-drum and miserable lives we were forced to live.

The company performed six nights and two matinees once every month at the Lyric Theatre in New Street and between times in various other venues such as the Regal Cinema, The North Cinema and also at Candie Gardens. Our shows were very popular and I am not quite sure who enjoyed them most, the audience or the players!

It was at about the time that we were exempt from being deported that the parents of the baritone in our company received notice that they must go. Douglas was a perfect singer with a voice like brown velvet. His mother, Mrs luckie got in touch with my mother and asked her if she would take Douglas in to live with us to avoid him having to go with them to a Camp. My parents readily agreed and the week they were due to leave, we were doing a show called "Cafe Continental" and before the final curtain fell we had a cafe scene on the stage, and just before the end Douglas had to stand up, pick up his glass of wine, and walking towards the footlights begin to sing "A Toast To Absent Friends". As rumors so rife at that time, most of the people in the audience knew that his parents had left the Island that day and were very moved as he sang. As the song neared its end, Douglas raised his glass to the audience and sang;

"So raise your glasses everyone, the toast is absent friends". Then he emptied his glass as the final curtain fell. We were so emotional on his behalf that we were shocked when the audience remained dead quiet, then as the curtain divided for him to take a bow, a voice from the very back of the auditorium shouted out;

"Don't worry Doug, they will soon be home again" and then the clapping began in earnest. Whistles, cheering, then more clapping; the audience just went wild. They wanted an encore, but Dougie was too overcome to sing again, so when the orchestra began to play, we all stood up and sang the final chorus for him, not an easy task when one is choked with emotion!

Gwen and I had recently acquired crystal set radios which it was strictly forbidden for use by the locals, but we kept ours very carefully hidden, but when we went to bed at night we would lock the door and the settle ourselves down to listen to the BBC. Gwen, who was the gifted pianist of the two of us would take down the music of any new songs we felt we could use at the Lyric, and I would take down the words I remember one song in particular being sung by Vera Lynne called "My sister and I". It was about two little Dutch girls who had to evacuate because of the war and was so reminiscent of our recent loss of so many little Island children that we just knew we must learn it. My sister looked at me with one eyebrow raised, and I at once nodded furiously. She took down the music and I the words, and after a few days of practice, we were ready to sing it in the next show.

Well, the terrific ovation that we received proved how very many of the audience had crystal sets or radios hidden in their homes, and realised that we did too!!

I think perhaps the Germans making up part of the audience wondered why such a simple little tune could warrant such applause.

As commanded, my father duly presented himself to the Rockmount Hotel to begin his forced labour! The German in charge was a member of the Organisation Todt known as the O.T's. He was a huge man, both in height, width and manner and with a voice to match and believe it or not, his name was Amen Krist.

My father and he felt an animosity towards one another from the start and it did not improve when it became known that while he was in charge of five coppers used to cook food for the forced labour people, my father was to be in charge of the remaining five.

Whilst for the first day or two they were engaged in boiling cabbage my father noticed many sacks of rice standing in the far corner of the very large room. He noticed also that the bottoms of most of them were broken and had grains of rice together with rat or mice droppings spilling out. In another corner two unused coppers that had been cast aside as they had begun leaking.

Carefully scraping and brushing away the contaminated rice, he and his helpers carried several sacks to the broken coppers and tipped the rice into them.

Amen Krist immediately rushed across to my father's area and asked what was going on.

"This rice is going to waste so I am going to add it to the cabbage in my soup".

"For what purpose?" asked the German.

"To give a little more sustenance to the starving souls who have to eat it", came the reply.

"Who gave you permission so to do?" he asked in his broken English.

"I am taking it upon myself to try to prolong life for a little longer for some poor hungry souls".

"You are mad, you should be careful to prolong your own life, you won't, if you keep doing things like that without permission, I would sooner let the rodents that come at night eat their fill than give good food to the scum brought over as labour".

Father was too angry to speak so ignored him and carried on adding ladles of rice to the cabbage water.

My mother knew at once that something was wrong when dad walked in from work that night and when she asked him, he told her about the rice. She warned him about getting into trouble through Krist, but he told her not to worry he would be careful.

Several weeks and disputes later, some beef was brought to the Hotel to be used in the soup. Dad was overjoyed and began to sharpen his butcher's knife on his steel. Immediately Krist was beside him.

" What do you think you are going to do Smith, don't you dare touch that meat, I am planning to use it for my men".

"It is not for your men, they have their own rations, this has been sent to us to be used in the soup" dad argued, "and into my soup it is going".

Before he could touch the beef, Krist grabbed the knife out of my father's hand.

"Stop it you filthy English swine" yelled Krist.

It was then that dad finally lost his temper.

"Right you German filth, you have been asking for this for a long time, and it might interest you to know that I am not English, I am a true Scot, born and bred in Scotland".

My father came from a family of six boys who had learned to fight as a pack with no holds barred, and to add to that he had been a butcher for many years and was used to carrying whole sides of beef and very large pigs bodies on his shoulders, so he had muscles of iron.

He suddenly lunged at Amen Krist catching him in the stomach, and as he folded forward on to dad's shoulder, my father swung him off his feet, and crossing the room dumped him headfirst into one of the empty coppers leaving him with his legs in the air in the sign of "V" for victory, and with that dad grabbed his coat and made for home.

We were all very surprised to see him home so early and when he explained why my poor mother was beside herself with fear.

"You can be shot for that" she whimpered.

"Do you think I don't know that" he heaved a great sigh, " we will just have to wait and see".

So we waited, and we waited but bed time came around and no one called.

The next morning we were all sitting quietly eating, or pretending to eat our breakfast when we heard the dreaded sound of jackboots on the gravel.

"This is it", somebody said.

Without knocking, the door was opened followed by the kitchen door, and there stood the Officer in Charge of the Kitchens.

"Why are you here Smith?" he asked, "You should have been at the Hotel half an hour ago".

"I thought after what happened yesterday I would not be expected".

The German laughed, "if you only knew we have all wanted to do what you did many, many times but no one had the courage or the strength to do it, now come on, there is work to be done", and saluting my mother he led dad out of the kitchen.

We waited on tender hooks for father's return to know what happened when he got to the Hotel.

Amen Krist was waiting for them with his hand outstretched. Krist said he was sorry and he had no idea that dad was not an Englishman and in this new knowledge he hoped they would be friends in the future. My father, never one to bear a grudge took his hand and shook it, and while it was possible the soup got stronger and had much more flavour to it.

I was now fifteen coming up sixteen, and as I was leaving childhood behind, I began to want to do something with my life, but what? To travel was out of the question, so what could I do to relieve the boredom in my life?

Two of my best friends were nurses at the Emergency hospital situated near our home, they suggested I apply for a position there and when I pointed I was not quite sixteen yet, they both laughed and said,

"Well lie, you look eighteen anyway, and Matron is desperate for nurses".

So I applied and was granted an interview with the Matron of the hospital the following Monday. I arrived at the specified time and was terrified by the Matron who greeted me into her office.

She was the most awesome lady I had ever met, and made the school teachers I had been afraid of seem like pussycats.

The interview, thankfully was quite short, and when she asked me my age I just said I would soon be eighteen. She looked up from her desk and I did not flinch for a second but I knew from her expression that she did not believe me. However, she told me the hours I would be expected to work, what the wages would be, and that I would be billeted in a farmhouse at the far end of the hospital meadow. She told me to talk it over with my parents, visit the farmhouse with them and then let her know my decision. If it was favourable, I must supply a uniform, whether begged, borrowed or stolen from an ex-nurse, and be ready for duty on the first of the following month.

The next difficult thing to do was to tell my parents what I had done! The objections were almost insurmountable but I was like a dog with a bone and they began to realise my mind was made up. So the next thing to do was visit the farmer and his wife where I would be staying. They were real old Guernsey people and already had two nurses living there already, I took to them immediately and they to me, I think.

At last the great day arrived and when I made my appearance at the porter's lodge, I was sent up to the Surgical wards, where I stayed until the day I finally left. The medical and maternity wards had their own staff and we did not change over duties. The first thing the other nurses did was show me how to make up my butterfly cap, and after putting it on my head, I was sent down the female ward to sister who was waiting for me in the sluice. On my way there I could see my shadow cast on the wall to my right, gosh, my cap was something else, I felt like a second Florence Nightingale, and swaggered along.

When I reached the third bed, a voice murmured "Nurse, I need a bed pan", I faced her and put on my most sympathetic smile and nodding said;

"I'll fetch a nurse".

Walking swiftly back to the duty room, I poked my head around the door and said:

"The lady in bed three needs a bedpan", to which the answer came in unison-

"Well get her one!!"

So my nursing days had begun, and I was just me, not Florence Nightingale after all.

I was quite surprised to find that I fitted in pretty quickly, and really enjoyed my work.

My first shift on night duty was something else. For one thing the electricity was cut off at nine o'clock and we had to spend the night in the dark. We had candles, but the supply was dwindling dangerously so we could only use them in an emergency. The nights seemed to be endless, the staff would sit in the duty room in total darkness and every now and again Sister would speak to one or the other of us to make sure we were awake. Now and again someone would begin to snore and the nurse next to her would give her a poke in the ribs to wake her up. From time to time Sister would call someones name and that nurse would light the candle and do a round of the ward, that usually came as relief, it was so nice to get moving.

The months rolled slowly by and I learned an awful lot, even spending short spells in the operating Theatre I which really enjoyed. The most upsetting thing I had to do was lay out my first patient who had died. She was a lovely gentle lady, a half negress with pure white tight curls all over her head, but the most startling thing about her was that she had bright blue eyes, the bluest eyes I had ever seen. Being the first time, I was assisting a senior nurse and pretending that it was having no impression on me at all but I was shaking inside, and when we turned her on to her front to wash her back, her lungs emptied and she exhaled a long and low groan. I leapt back from the bed,

"She is still alive ", I gasped.

My colleague smothered a giggle and explained what had really happened, "she is dead all right " she said and we continued to wash her back. Carefully we turned her on to her back and to my horror one of her eyes had opened and she was staring up at me with one bright blue eye! My heart skipped quite a few beats before I could continue with my work.

I had to repeat this sad office many times before I was allowed to be in charge and have a more junior nurse to assist me.

The first time I had to officiate in charge at such a sad occasion was when I was on night duty.

My lovely lady passed away about two o'clock in the morning and it was my duty to perform the last offices of the dead on her. Of course I had to work most of the time in the dark, but a male nurse from the other ward came to assist me and had a cigarette lighter with him which he lit when I really needed light. The fuel in the lighter was eau-de-cologne which his mother had given him from her own supply, and it therefore gave only a pale blue shadow of light but was better than nothing to serve the purpose for which it was needed.

I brought the tray I had got ready and put it on the patient's locker. The other nurse lit his lighter while I got what I needed from her locker. Then as he extinguished the light I dipped her flannel into the bowl of warm water and taking her soap from the saucer in which it was lying I began to rub it on her flannel, all in pitch darkness! I could feel no sense of lather, so tried again. I knew the soap that we were getting from France was rubbish, a wet bar had once been left on a chair at my uncle's house and not noticing it he sat down on it. The result was that my aunt never did succeed in removing the stain. I smiled to myself in the dark and tried the soap on the flannel again, no lather, so I shrugged my shoulders and began the task of giving my lady her last wash. Every now and again the lighter was lit to help me on my way until at last I had finished, and the porters wheeled the trolley in to take my patient down to the mortuary.

We buried our dead very quickly in those days because the rat community were as hungry as we were, so under ground was the safest place for them!

When I reported to Sister that I had completed my task, she told me to wait to clear up until dawn when I would be able to see what I was doing; I was more than pleased to obey.

As soon as it was light enough I went to the ward and began to strip the bed. I next emptied her locker ready to put her belongings into a bag for her relatives to take home. Imagine my horror when I brought out the saucer with her soap on it. I stared unbelieving at it and could not believe my eyes. I had been washing her with her cheese ration!!!

We Can Take It
Poem wrote circa 1943

The have called in our rifle, our wireless, sword and gun,

As oppressors they're within their rights I'm sure

And being truly British, we've complied with their demands

And we haven't got these items any more.

Last night as mother baked, they turned the gas off from the mains,

So off to bed she went in such a rage,

Then this morning as the lethal fumes came creeping back again,

Our canaries both were gassed within their cage.

They're killing off our animals, they're pilfering our fields

They're demoralizing everything in site;

But then again, that's feasible, we know, we understand,

As the victors, then of course they have the right.

So we cringe in mild submission, and we bow to their demands

They can shoot the population if they choose;

What they don't know is beneath my bed there is a crystal set

And the BBC's still giving us the news.

When they searched for weapons , all the house was upside down,

But the underground had warned us, what a laugh!

So they did not find my crystal set, or Father's sword and gun

They were safe behind the panels 'round the bath.

They can take all our possessions, steal our cats and dogs as well,

Mental torment is their speciality,

But there's one thing they can never have, no matter how they try,

That's our upper stiff lip British dignity.

*The Lyric No. 1 company who put on a show every month during
the occupation at :-
Lyric Theatre, Regal Cinema, North Cinema, Candie Gardens*

*"Four Hits and a Miss"
The band who entertained to
bring happiness to lighten the
dark days.*

'MUM'
MIRIAM SMITH
1940 - 1945
Just before and just after
The Occupation of our Island by German Troops!

Miss Betts in bottom centre who was hit by the train

Harbour

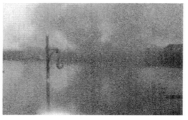

Weighbridge   *Aftermath of the bombing*

Devastation caused by the German bombs

Occupation forces in St. Peter Port

Swastika flying in front of our Crown Hotel

When all was peaceful, when life had just begun

Aged 3 years   *The Smith Twins*

With Rupert and Cedric our two St. Bernard dogs

*Outfits made in the tartan of our
father's clan*

In the uniforms that were made for us when we were invited to take tea in the admiral's cabin aboard the H.M.S. Hood when she visited Guernsey

When it was all over, the nursing training began at Bromley & District Hospital

Chapter 6.

The worst day of the whole of the occupation however, had nothing to do with the Germans as such.

Our hotel, "Les Pieux," had several large lawns on three sides of the building; the one at the back was lower than the house and was reached by cement steps. At the far end of this area my parents had had six wooden chalets built to accommodate extra holiday makers, and these rooms had been commandeered by the enemy to provide shelter for forced labour members. They had their own entrance and never came near where we lived, which was a great relief as they were a motley crew of humans with a nefarious streak.

One afternoon my mother, my sister and I were alone in the kitchen when we heard a terrific bang outside the house. Going to the window we saw one of the men walking crookedly back along the lawn then he turned, and running as fast as his drunken state would allow, he made a b-line for one of the doors and head butted it like a goat at a fence. The sound was frightening, we all gasped and mum uttered, "He'll kill himself in a minute."

Undaunted, however, he returned across the lawn and repeated the procedure.

"Stupid man, he is going to knock himself out in a minute", but as he turned around to do it once again, he spotted us all in the window and made towards the steps that would bring him to our level.

"Into the utility room, quick" commanded our frightened parent," get under the sink, hurry." So we fell to our knees and crawled under the large old-fashioned stone sink. We could hear him mumbling and swearing in French outside the window that we were hiding beneath. This went on for a considerable length of time, then at last, all was quiet.

We waited for what seemed a terrible long time, and then my mother looked at me and whispered, "You are the closest, get up slowly and see if he is around".

At first I was a little nervous and hesitated," go on, but do it gently" urged Mum.

Very slowly I got on to my knees, then slipping my hands over the top of the sink I pulled myself slowly upwards. As my eyes slowly focused over the top I found myself looking into a pair of staring blood shot eyes the other side of the glass in the window.

With a muffled cry escaping my lips I sank back down on to the floor.

"He's there" I managed to gasp and I could feel each beat of my heart as if it was vibrating in my throat, I could hardly breathe, "he'll break the window for sure" I managed to splutter.

It was at this moment that we heard voices and realised more of the workers had returned home and were out searching for him. They found him and as they shouted at him in French he began to fight them. We then had the courage to climb from our hiding place and rushed to the window to see what was going to happen.

They half dragged, half carried him to the steps then threw him down them on to the lower lawn. They followed in a bunch and jumping on top of him began to hit and punch him. I saw one of the men pick up a large boulder from the garden with a great deal of difficulty, and raising it with shaking hands got ready to bash it down on his face. At that precise moment I heard my father's strong voice shouting;

"What exactly is going on here?"

Suddenly there was dead silence, then a spokesman explained that the man was drunk and as always in that, situation was out of control.

"That gives you no reason to kill the man" continued dad in a strong and controlled voice, "here, someone help me to get him to his room" and he started to lift the now unconscious man to an upright position. Suddenly there was a rush of volunteers to help, while several went on ahead to show my father which room he occupied, and having deposited him inside they locked the door and left him to sleep it off.

We, the female members of the family, were badly shaken and it was several days before we got over the incident, just in time as it happened before another calamity prevailed.

Two young French brothers in their twenties shared the room at the end of the chalets. They kept themselves very much to themselves, but were always polite if they came face to face with any of my family.

When dad returned from work one cold and miserable evening he had a sad story to tell.

The two young brothers had had a very bad argument at the hotel, which had ended in a fight, and the elder of the brothers had grabbed a carving knife from the table and stabbed his brother.

"Is he badly injured? " my mother wanted to know.

This question was met with silence for a few minutes, and then in a quiet voice my father said "he is dead".

My mother clapped her hand over her mouth "what has happened to the other one?" she mumbled through her fingers?"

"Well when he realised what he had done, he dropped to his knees and lifting his brother up, nursed him like a baby and the tears just rolled uncontrollably down his cheeks. They finally lifted the dead boy from his arms and they have locked him up in the little hut at the bottom of the Guet where he will stay until a boat comes to take him away to France";- my mother interrupted here and said it could take days and he would freeze to death during the night.

"Get me a blanket and some food, and I will take them to him" said Dad.

Mother got together what she could spare, which was not much, and Dad set off on his journey.

In those days, unlike now, the slats in the little window of the door were quite wide apart. No one was in sight so father looked through at the young boy. He rushed forward when he saw who it was.

Putting his tear stained face to the bars, he asked "is my brother all right, I did not really hurt him did I".

Dad ignored this question and began to put the corner of the blanket between the bars with orders to pull from the other side, and pushing and pulling together they eventually got the blanket through, followed by what little food there was.

"Thank you very much, and please thank your wife too, and please tell me, is my brother all right?"

"I am afraid the knife went deeper than you meant it to, and he has since died from his wounds".

The boy's expression turned to one of horror, and he burst into tears, sobbing "I did not want to hurt him, I was angry and I lost my temper, I love him and would never hurt him" and he burst into a fresh bout of sobbing and as much as he wanted to, there was nothing my father could do to help him, so he just walked away.

Father returned the next day as soon as it was daylight, the door was wide open, and the little hut was empty, but our blanket was neatly folded in the far corner, albeit slightly damp at one edge from tears.

It was about at this time that things began to really tighten up.

The following orders appeared in the Press.

"All bread deliveries will cease on July 13th. The rate of exchange to become fixed at 7 Reich marks per pound.

All expectant mothers must obtain admission to the Emergency Hospital for confinements as no doctors or nurses will be allowed to attend private homes after curfew.

Horse buses will provide transport to and from St. Sampson's and St. Peter Port.

All dealers in clothing and footwear required to furnish the States Committee with an inventory of their stock.

Tree felling will start on Thursday to replace coal supplies.

A census of Pigeons will take place and all birds to be kept in their loft and not allowed to fly freely.

All potatoes on abandoned properties to be the sole property of the States.

Paraffin sales to cease on Saturday.

Those living near bake houses are urged to use their services to cook food for the family."

Then as an obvious ploy to catch any one who had disobeyed the order to turn in their radio sets there was an advert worded like this.

"Wanted to buy: Portable Radio in good condition. Reply either in writing or in person to give particulars of price required. Apply, The German Commandant's Office."

"There is a need for drastic economy in everything, stocks are rapidly shortening. A problem vital to the Island.

The Royal Court has passed an ordinance making talk against German Authorities punishable. As the Control Committee are now asking for real sacrifice it is only right and proper that the public should be kept informed of the situation so that they may appreciate its importance and implications and act accordingly."

Which reminds me of the radio we had hidden in the cellar of our home. We had very large cellars at Les Pieux, a large room beneath each room above it. These rooms could be reached through a trap door in the floor of a linen cupboard, which was naturally kept covered with various things such as an ironing board and various other items of laundry equipment.

Every night just before 6 o'clock my father would make sure the coast was clear and then vanish into the linen cupboard and down into the cellar to hear our English news. This of course was at the risk of being shot if he was caught.

One night in particular just before 6 o'clock, the back door opened followed by the kitchen door and in walked one of the soldiers who was bat man to one of the officers in the house. He pulled out a chair and sat down without even being invited.

"What can we do for you?" my mother asked; but before he had time to answer, we all heard it. It was little more than a muffled sound, but anyone familiar with it knew instantly it was the tones of Big Ben!

My mother suddenly began to talk in a very loud voice whilst banging her foot on the floor. Gwen and I began to argue very loudly and the German stared from one of us to the other with a puzzled expression on his face.

"Maybe I have come at the wrong time" he said, standing up, "I will come another time," and with this he left the house.

"You wait till I get hold of your father" threatened my trembling mother, "that stupid radio will be the death of us yet, the times I have told him to get rid," but we had had yet another close escape and only one of many more to come!

Another one of these frightening occasions happened one night when it was our turn to have the use of the lounge. We had invited a few friends around and intended to have a musical evening. Dad opened the dividing doors between the dining-room and the lounge turning them into one large long room. Our upright piano stood at the far end of the dining-room, and the grand piano was in the bay window of the lounge. Gwen and I started the evening off each seated at a piano and we had a lovely sing-song for several hours. There was something very satisfying to be able to sing ones heart out at this terrible time of our lives.

We then played gramophone records and danced with each other until we tired of that; and that was when someone suggested dancing the Siegfried Line dance. Did we dare, with so many Germans in the building?

The words of the song went like this;-

"We're going to hang our washing on the Siegfried Line, Have you any dirty washing mother dear?

We're going to hang our washing on the Siegfried Line, 'cos our washing day is here.

Whether the weather may be wet or fine, we'll just rub along without a care.

We're going to hang our washing on the Siegfried Line, if the Siegfried Line's still there."

We would stand in a line and whilst singing these words we would march down the room doing the goose step with our right arm out in the Nazi salute, while we would hold one finger of our left hand under our nose to imitate Hitler's moustache.

When we got to the end of the room we would return in the same style.

We were going back for about the fourth time when our friend who was playing the piano stopped and the music ceased. We stayed still and I noticed everyone was staring at the door behind us. I turned and froze in horror, because there in the doorway stood two of the officers from upstairs.

Chapter 7.

Our line of friends slowly split up, and the two Germans walked into the room.

"Dance that dance again" one of them ordered.

In terror I looked at my father.

"Do as they ask" he said.

So we went to the top of the room, sorted ourselves into a line, and as the piano began to play we started our singing albeit with a little less enthusiasm than before.

When we had finished, both the Germans stepped forward with huge grins on their faces, and were clapping their hands.

"Very, very funny, you see we Germans have a sense of humour too, now I want you to write the words down for me and you" pointing to Ernie at the piano "can you write music?" and when he nodded his head, was told "write down the notes for my comrade here, have them all ready for the morning". Then they both left the room.

We spent the next half hour or so doing as he had ordered us, and laughingly said we were probably signing our death warrants.

"They will probably forget all about it by morning" comforted my mother, but first thing the next day the talkative one appeared in the kitchen and asked for the papers.

"So now we will just have to wait and see".

No one used the lounge for the next few days, and then my father was informed that the Officers would be using it on the next evening.

They were pretty quiet, and I was just dozing off when I heard the strains of the piano wafting up from below, and what was it but the Siegfried Line tune followed almost immediately by the refrain chanted in broken English. I could hear the muffled sound of their feet as they marched up and down the room. I held my covers over my mouth to drown the sound of my laughter as I realised they did not get the full significance of the words.

They sang it over and over again to much laughing and clapping without realising they were making fun of their own nation, and if they were holding their fingers under their noses, making fun of their own Fuhrer.

Much hilarity was enjoyed over the next few months, and then came the time for the men in our home to be replaced by a new batch of officers, and as was the case for the rest of the occupation, each batch became more rough and uncouth, and as the months went by, we became more hungry and cold, no coal for the fires, and most of the spare furniture in the home had long since been burnt, and when the slightest thing went wrong tempers flayed on both sides.

Clothes were no longer in the shops and I personally was wearing my two gymslips cut down into skirts, my school blouses with the buttons moved as near to the edge as possible as I left behind the figure of a school girl. I had been provided with two dresses for 'best' wear made from some curtains packed away in the linen cupboard, and as my feet grew together with my body I was learning to walk in wooden clogs brought over from France.

The local newspaper told us that four airmen were killed and three wounded when a German plane was obliged to make a forced landing on our airport, causing damage to property and materials. We read also that also that a delayed action bomb dropped from an English plane had missed the airport and crashed on a greenhouse where it exploded and damaged the property. It was announced that civil inhabitants need not fear to work at the airport as there were now a number of fighter planes which would afford safety against attack.

An air raid siren was sounded yesterday followed by the all clear forty five minutes later, it was announced that the 'offensive plane kept at a very great height.

The last blackout offence to be treated by a fine has been heard. In future, all blackout offences will not be tolerated and will be met with imprisonment.

In the event of bombs or aircraft shells being discovered in this Island, the matter is to be reported immediately to the German Commandant, Channel Island Hotel, on no account should any civilian touch or approach near such bombs or shells.

All corn after threshing, must be sent to a central depot where it will be checked, weighed, and graded and paid for at a rate of fourteen shillings and sixpence per cwt for first rate, inferior quality at a reduced rate.

Farmers must NOT breed Alderney cattle.

Air raid shelters can be found at:-

Boots Chemist, High Street.

Entrance to Market Halls.

Albert Statue.

Moores Hotel.

Colonel Schumacher has opened a sub office in Guernsey. It is a military administration office (Nebenstelle) dealing with civilian matters especially with relation to the economic aspect. We are officially informed that this new sub office will be run by Dr. Wilhelm Raffler and will be opened at Grange Lodge in the course of the next few days.

Census figures of residents nearly halved by evacuation population:

MALES;	65 years and over	1,807
	64 to 19 years	8,067
	18 to 14 years	865
	13 to 6 years	460
	5 to 1 years	446
FEMALES:	60 years and over	2,931
	59 to 19 years	7,322
	18 to 14 years	843
	13 to 6 years	551
	5 to 1 years	469
BABIES	Under 1 year old	220

Even after all these months of near starvation the German troops still kept to their routine of daily route marches. They would march along singing with much gusto all their familiar marching songs, their favourite being "We're going to Eng-er –land". No matter whom the soldiers were or where they came from, they would sing in perfect harmony and more often than not they would be followed by small boys skipping and running and singing along with them. The children had heard the songs so often and in true childish fashion had picked up the words even 'though they did not have any idea what the words meant.

An article in a German newspaper at this time stated that by the strength of their Army, Navy and Air force, the Islands of Guernsey, Jersey, Alderney and Sark have been taken. This is the first time for 1,000 years that the islands have been invaded. The King of England is their Duke.

The industry of Guernsey, the article went on, is mostly tomatoes of which thousands of tons are exported to England monthly. On account of the occupation all this has been cut off, so it has now been decided to grow more potatoes, beans and other necessities. There are about 5,000 motor cars in Guernsey but only about 300 are in use, the others are laid up.

Policemen in Guernsey are called der Bobby.

The writer then commented on the "excellent terms which exist between the Islanders and the German Forces in occupation!!!"

In the local Press the following announcement appeared.

"In the course of an interview at Grange Lodge with Dr Wilhelm Raffler and Dr E. Mass this morning, Dr Mass made an important declaration which we have pleasure in placing before our readers.

Dr Mass said that since the beginning of the occupation every effort has been made to organise the provisioning of the Island. Naturally there has been a great difficulty. Difficulties which resulted chiefly from the destruction of communication in France and the lack of suitable tonnage.

There is on the Continent plenty of meat, flour, coal and the Islander public may be assured that the Feld Commandant will secure imports as need arises."

"Yeah, Whatever!!!!"

We were so excited when we heard that two Guernsey men who had joined the army at the beginning of the war, had landed on the Island and were in hiding from the Germans.

The girl friends of these men were known to us and through them we knew where the boys were hiding. Naturally it was a close secret. Several nights following the two hideaways arrived at the arranged rendezvous but the submarine that was supposed to pick them up did not surface, so they were trapped in enemy territory.

Eventually, the Germans tracked them down and they, together with their girl friends and all families concerned were sent to a prison called Cherche Midi in France. One of the girls did know her family had been interned, but one morning as she looked down at the exercise yard from the window of her cell she could not believe her eyes when she saw her father. Not being allowed to shout out to them she started to sing "Somewhere over the Rainbow" at the top of her voice, her father looked up and tears pouring down their cheeks they blew kisses to each other.

On Friday July 28th 1944 Graham Buckingham, a 24 year old local footballer and all round sportsman was being taken under German guard down the White Rock for deportation to France. He had been sentenced that morning for several thefts from the Germans and they were obviously eager to get him away from the Island as ships were few and far between. Suddenly he made a daring escape, he bent to tie his shoe lace and as the guard walked slowly on he turned and tore away up the White Rock .

He made his way to the Canichers, around to the Vauxlaurens, around Candie through the Croutes and away to Saints. Earlier on, he and his friend had made a canoe which they kept at St. Martins with a view to escaping from the Island.

Hoping to escape he made for the canoe which was now at Portinfer and intended to leave the Island from there, but the sea was too rough and a local fisherman strongly advised him not to try.

The next morning he looked up some friends in an attempt to get some food and received a very warm welcome. He remained with them for two months or so, until a quisling informed the Gestapo that his friends had a radio and Germans arrived to search the house. They did not find a radio, neither did they find Graham hidden in a loft above the kitchen!

When things got a bit hot there, Graham began to visit his family several times a week, until one night he had an accident, he fell on a broken bottle and received a bad injury which needed immediate medical attention, he was taken to the hospital where I was nursing, and kept on the top floor with a policeman on guard duty. He remained up there for several weeks, and then he was taken back to prison.

Our doctor argued with the Germans that he was unfit to travel to France and so he remained in Guernsey until the end of the war on conditions that he visited a local doctor twice a week under police escort.

Miss Betts was a lady in every true sense of the word, with only one exception, she was stone deaf. She lived alone in a little cottage at St. Sampsons and every morning through rain or shine she would walk into St.Peter Port where she worked in a photographer's studio. She was an artist and worked on all the negatives removing any blemishes before they were enlarged into portraits. On her way to work she had received many a close shave with large German lorries driving too close to the pavement and not being able to hear them had been brushed aside but thankfully not hurt.

One morning in particular she was walking gracefully along, head up, shoulders back, feet turned out at ten to two and decided to walk in the railway track to avoid the lorries rushing along the road. She had done this ever since the Germans had built a railway track all around the Island's coast to transport cement, boulders and workers to various places to build their monstrosities known as bunkers in an effort to protect themselves from invasion!

This morning in particular the train was late and as Miss Betts glided gracefully along it puffed slowly along in the distance. As it drew nearer, it sounded its whistle. Miss Betts heard nothing and kept on walking. This was repeated twice, and then the driver must have concluded that some stupid Guernsey woman was doing it deliberately to obstruct the train. With one final warning whistle the train shunted forward and hit Miss Betts sending her flying forward on to the track and knocking her unconscious on the line.

The horse drawn ambulance (no petrol) galloped up and took her to Hospital, but her injuries were few and she soon returned home, just very, very shocked.

TO BE SUNG TO THE TUNE OF JINGLE BELLS
Poem wrote circa 1943

Bramble tea, bramble tea,

Brambles all the way,

Oh what fun it is to drink

In this unusual way;

Have another slice,

Oh what fun to fill oneself

Even if the taste's not nice.

Eating all we can, never mind the taste,

Everything goes down, nothing goes to waste;

Most folk eat a peck of dirt before they die,

We're all set to eat a ton, why, oh why, oh why?

Seaweed pud, seaweed pud,

Never mind the sand,

Oh what fun when need and greed

Both go hand in hand.

Use your jaws, chomp and chew,

All flavours will rescind,

Why worry ? in no time at all

It's all gone with the wind!

Chapter 8.

Josef Long was an officer and a gentleman despite the offensive uniform he was destined to wear. He spoke the King's English to perfection, and it was rumoured that he had attended Oxford University before the war began. I had met him a few times in our house and knew that he was a first class horseman and had a horse named Freda.

One afternoon I was enjoying the day off duty and was lying on the front lawn of our house with Gwen, sunbathing. As no one was around we were both in our bathing-costumes. I was dozing and although I had my eyes closed I was only half asleep. I was vaguely aware of movement but took no notice until a shadow closed my face which made me open my eyes. There to my horror was an enormous horse standing beside me and on its back sat Jo. I began to sit up but he stopped me.

"Do not move one iota" he ordered "just keep absolutely still and Freda will perform for you".

With that he walked closer and speaking to his horse in German, the two of them came right up close to me.

Then Freda lifted one hoof and I felt it glide across my midriff, followed swiftly by another. I could scarcely breath I was so frightened. The third hoof pressed a little closer to me and I was in dread of what the fourth one would do. I need not have concerned myself; she lifted the fourth hoof higher than the others and walked away from me.

I sat up with all speed in case Jo would repeat the performance, but he turned his horse to face me, and jumping from its back said:-

"Now, bow for the lovely English lady Freda" and as he touched her gently on her withers with his whip she stretched one front leg forward, and slid her face down to her hoof in a most graceful bow. As she straightened up, Jo sprang into the saddle and Freda trotted along the drive towards the gate, Jo touched his cap with his crop in a salute then they disappeared from view and I heard the clip clop of her hooves as they galloped along the road and away.

****

The next time I saw Josef, it was under very different circumstances.

My family and I were enjoying a quiet cup of some sort of mint tea which my mother had managed to get in exchange for a pair of shoes my sister had grown out of. The door burst open and there stood Jo with a face as white as a sheet and swollen eyes which looked as though they had cried a river of tears.

"Good grief man, whatever is the matter?" asked my father, "for goodness sake sit down, it can't be that bad"

"It is. Oh it is" said Jo as he sat on the edge of the sofa, "it is my Freda" and with this he drew a handkerchief from his pocket, and burying his face in it began to sob pitifully.

"Who on earth is Freda" I heard my father whisper to my mother. She raised her shoulders and sighed.

"That is his horse" I said.

"Thank goodness for that" said Dad," I thought he had had bad news from home".

"Oh it is bad news all right, let me tell you what has happened" interrupted Jo.

He blew his nose vigorously then putting his handkerchief back into his pocket, he began his tale of woe.

"It was such a lovely day when I awoke this morning that I decided to exercise my horse, Freda, before starting my duties for the day.

We walked slowly along the coast enjoying the lovely sea breeze that came wafting up from the beach, Freda was anxious to break into a run, but I held her back until we would reach our destination.

On and on we walked, and on and on she shook her head eager to get galloping. Eventually we reached our destination – L'Ancresse Common, and as there were only a few soldiers walking idly around I decided to let Freda have her head.

Giving her a gentle kick in the ribs and clicking my tongue we were away. Faster and faster we galloped, I shook my head in the wind and thought what a lovely day it was. Several of the soldiers gave a whoop of joy as we galloped past, and I acknowledged their praise with a salute.

All was too well with my world, I should have known something would go amiss, and suddenly it did! As Freda went faster and faster I decided to curb her exuberance a little and was just about to pull her up when it happened!

She caught her hoof in a pothole and tumbled forward with a terrific force that sent me flying from her back on to the common. I was completely dazed for a second or two, and then as I got my wits together I saw my lovely Freda lying on the grass. She was whinnying loudly and then I noticed it. Her front leg was jotting out at a most horrific angle, and as I struggled to get up and go to her I knew without a doubt her leg was broken.

By the time I reached her several of the soldiers I had passed before were already standing near her, I sat on the grass and lifted her beautiful head on to my knee. I was stroking her face when I noticed one of the soldiers was my sergeant and he knelt down beside me.

'You know her leg is broken 'he said 'and that means only one thing'. I knew he was making sense but I could not possibly take it on board. By this time Freda had stopped whinnying and was making deep guttural grunts.

'She is suffering, do the kind thing and put her out of her misery' said my sergeant, and I knew it had to be done. I pulled my legs from under her head and laying it gently on the grass I stood up.

I then noticed my sergeant was getting his revolver out of its holster.

I stopped him at once, and told him it was my responsibility. I then removed my own pistol; I first knelt down and whispered to Freda that soon the pain would be gone, then standing up I pointed my gun towards her lovely forehead, and pulled the trigger.

As the shot echoed across the bay I felt Freda's spirit flying away with it. She was out of pain at last. I left my sergeant with orders to see to her body which he was only too pleased to do, then I walked away before they saw the tears that were falling fast."

With a tear rolling slowly down his cheek, Jo tried to smile." I expect you thought that soldiers were too hard to cry" he said My father patted Jo's shoulder and said "Anyone who can love an animal like you did must have a heart, so must be able to shed tears too".

Eventually Jo succeeded in pulling himself together and thanking my parents shook hands and left I was absolutely devastated at the thought of that beautiful horse ending its life so soon. I could not sleep that night remembering how she had stepped so gently over me as I lay on the grass such a short time ago, and now she was gone, life was so unfair.

 Many weeks passed and we saw no more of Jo, my mother was anxious that he felt he had made a fool of himself in front of English people but my father pooh-poohed that idea, and he was right because several days later we heard it on the grapevine that Jo had been sent to Russia. Weeks later more news on the grapevine, Jo had been killed in action on the Russian Front.

So Jo is with his Freda at last. They can gallop over the clouds at will – Free spirits together once again.

****

This was a very bad time for rumours; some true, but some merely hearsay, I remember a few of them:- It was said that 500,000 eggs had been commandeered by German troops.

German troops tried to take away a Guernsey cow in an aero plane, but as she only stood in halfway they relinquished the idea, and took two small heifers instead.

Many pigs have also been removed by 'plane by the enemy troops.

Large quantities of food stuff have been shipped to France.

A large amount of leaflets have been dropped by English 'planes on L'Ancresse Common, local residents are forbidden to pick any up. (Oh Yeah).

The local potato crop is badly diseased.

The aerodrome is now covered with tree trunks to prevent enemy [English] 'planes from landing.

Such rumours as these caused a great deal of distress and anxiety especially to the elderly.

This was about the time when a copy of a speech made by His Majesty's Procurer in Guernsey just after the beginning of the Occupation, speaking to the people of the United Kingdom, and in particular those who had evacuated to the Mainland preceding the German Occupation, and then I quote:

"I imagine that many of you must be greatly worried as to how we are getting on. Well let me tell, some will fear, I imagine, I am making this record with a revolver pointed at my head and speaking from a typed script thrust into my hand by a German Officer.

The actual case is very different. The Lieutenant Governor and Bailiff Mr. Vic Carey, and every other Island official have been, and is being treated with every consideration and with the greatest courtesy by the German Military Authorities. The Island Government is functioning. Churches and Chapels are open for public worship. Banks, shops, and places of entertainment are open as usual.

The sudden and entire severance of communication with the United Kingdom created innumerable problems with which we have wrestled, and are still wrestling.

The States have set up a controlling committee to speed up public business. My friends, Sir Abraham Laine, A.M. Drake, R.O. Falla, R.H. Johns, Stamford Raffles, and Doctor A.N. Symons are collaborating with me on this committee and are working like Trojans. The conduct of the German forces is exemplary, I am proud of the way my fellow Islanders, and grateful for the correct and kindly attitude towards them of the German soldiers. We have always been, and still remain loyal subjects of his Majesty, and this has been made clear to and is respected by the German Commandant and his staff.

On that staff is an officer speaking perfect English, a man of wide experience with whom I am in daily contact, to him I express my grateful thanks for his courtesy and patience.

He then went on to mention various Island schools, teachers and pupils sending them all our love and good wishes, to all wives mothers and sweethearts, God bless you. To all Guernsey children in England. God keep you safe and bless you all till we meet again.

 Will the BBC please retransmit this message and will the Daily papers please publish it."

As it was the first time the Guernsey public had known about such a message, and the occupation was well into its third year, if not its fourth, anger ran high and several cartoons of the sender of this message hanging from a tree, with a caption suggesting that was what would happen after the war, were sent via the GUNS [Guernsey Underground Newspaper Service], but all was forgiven in the excitement of being freed many years later.

On one afternoon in particular I was off duty from two till four in the afternoon, so I decided to visit my family. As time was so short I did not want to waste it going back to my 'digs' to change into mufti, so taking off my cap, I put my cape around my shoulders, and after crossing the red straps along my chest and fastening them behind my back, I fastened the two hooks at my throat and made my way down to the bicycle shed.

Bicycles had been in use for so many years now that the materials needed to repair punctures had long been used up, so someone had come up with the great idea of replacing useless tyres with a length of hosepipe. This idea was great but I must admit it made cycling very much harder on the legs, and every time you ran over the join in the hosepipe there was a jolt, and I suspect that was the origin of the expression "saddle sore"!!

I jumped on my bike and peddled through the hospital gate and made my way towards the L'Aumone and home. I decided to avoid the coast road as I guessed a German patrol would be on duty, and made my way along Bouverie lane and used the back entrance to my house, by doing so I did not see the large important looking car parked in the front drive.

I leaned my bicycle against the wall and as I entered the back door I heard a man's loud voice shouting in the kitchen. I entered that room to find a member of the 'Geheimfeldpolizei' German Secret Police shouting at my mother.

"What's going on?" I queried. "Who are you?" shouted the German.

"This is my daughter" and I could hear the relief in her voice that I was there.

The German then turned his attention to me and asked "Where were you last evening?"

"I had a day off duty and I stayed here with my parents until just before curfew".

My lovely dog was prancing and jumping around me so pleased to see me at home.

"Who else was here?" the interrogation continued.

"Just me and my family".

"Your family being?"

"My father, my mother, my sister, and me".

"Who else was here" the interrogation continued.

"Just me and my family".

"Your family being"?

"My father, my mother, my sister and me".

"Ah, but your father was not here was he?"

"Indeed he was".

"You are lying, you are a liar, we know where your father was, he was at Grandes Rocques stealing food from the German depot".

"He was doing no such thing, he was here with us".

Suddenly he dragged a chair towards me shouting "SIT" as one might say to a dog in training it to be obedient. The command was such that as I obeyed, so did my dog who plonked down on the floor beside me. The German drew up another chair and sat in front of me, his knees almost touching mine. I could see that after interrogating my mother and then me, his patience was fast running out.

"Now let us start again, you, your mother and sister were here with you, just the three of you".

"Daddy was here too".

"No, we know differently, you must not lie to a German Officer".

"I am telling the truth" I insisted.

"I am fast loosing my temper, tell me the truth at once, and where was you father?"

"I am telling you the truth, he was here with us".

It was then that he reached to his side and pulled his revolver out of its holster and pointed it at my face.

"Now will you tell me the truth?"

I have never been so terrified in all my life. My throat felt as if it was swelling up, I could hardly swallow, my mouth was so dry my tongue seemed to be stuck to the roof of it, and my body temperature felt as if it was at boiling point. I stared down the barrel of that gun and in my minds eye could almost see the bullet flying down towards me. With trembling hands, I managed to grip the edges of my cape and flung them over my shoulders displaying the red cross of the straps.

Straight away I saw the devils expression change and giving me a final stare he stood up with such speed he sent his chair crashing to the floor and for a moment I thought the bang was the gun going off. He thrust the pistol back into its holster and heading for the door promised, "I'll be back, never fear".

As he opened the door, my dog leapt into action thinking it was time for a walk and the German banged it shut hitting my poor dog's nose. He sprang back with a terrible yelp, and when I rushed forward to comfort him, I saw two of his baby teeth lying on the floor.

I turned to my mother, "What made him change his mind, why am I not dead?" I asked, and my mother said then, and vowed to her dying day that it was the red cross of my straps on my white apron that saved my life. The Red Cross!

Mother and I held each other in a trembling embrace, and as it was getting near the time to return to my duties, mum suggested that I ring Matron and tell her of my ordeal. I felt it would all be in vain, but I did as mother asked. I was amazed at Matron's sympathy, she gave me two days compassionate leave and it was during these two days that the truth came out about the robbery.

Having heard us call my father Daddy the closest the Germans could get to that was "Tetti", and he became known as that by quite a few of the soldiers around the district.

It appeared that when the robbery was taking place, the robbers were interrupted by German soldiers, and as one man made his escape, he shouted out;

"Get out quick, the Huns are here, Teddy, come on". So this was how my father came to be involved. To our great relief, a Quisling from Grandes Rocques went to the German Commandant with a view to hopefully getting a reward and told him who the two culprits were, one being a Teddy Le Page, and gave his address. They immediately raided this mans house and found large quantities of German cigarettes and tinned food.

The tell-tale person was not rewarded, because as a German once told my father, we appreciate it when people come to us with information, but we despise the person who has told tales on a neighbour!

So another crisis was laid to rest, but in that day and age, it could only make room for another to arise.

****

One young soldier entered the room where my family and I were sitting one afternoon. He had his girl friend with him, not the usual cheap Gerry bag type, but a quiet pretty girl with a foreign accent. They were waiting for an officer who lived at Les Pieux and asked if they could sit down as she was expecting the soldier's baby. We were a little taken aback by his bluntness, but they waited quite a long time and obviously wanted to chat. It was very sad for her because he was due to go away the next day and he was worried for her being on her own.

Eventually their friend arrived and they stood up to leave. All my mother's maternal instincts rose to the fore, holding out her hand she said;

"As you have no relatives in Guernsey, if you need any help at all you know where I am".

The girl took my mother's hand in both of hers, and with tears in her eyes answered;

"I'll remember".

Unhappily, she did not, and being alone with no one to turn to, as her baby grew inside her she began to fear the future, to such an extent that she could bear no more.

For many days we heard no more of her, and then the news got to us that when her lover left the Island she returned alone to her little flat.

She removed the shelves from her oven, put a cushion on its base, then turning on the gas she got on to the floor, laid her head on the cushion, and closed her eyes.

After several deep breathes her soul soared to the realms above her sorrow, and of course she took her tiny German baby with her!

Ring a Ring of Roses
Poem wrote circa 1945

Ring-a-ring o' roses we all fall down'

'Jerry in the middle' is the game,

What happened to the piggy? He got eaten up

And Jerry is the bastard who's to blame.

Ring-a-ring o' roses we all fall down'

Each day we're weaker than the day before;

Our spirits are nearly broken, we're so sorry for ourselves,

And we don't play games of hoping anymore.

Ring-a-ring o' roses we all fall down'

Grannies, babies, fathers mums and all;

And if this bloody was doesn't hurry up and end,

There won't be any people left to fall.

Chapter 9.

The food situation had now become critical; it was not too bad at first because we could get food from the sea. My father had bought a crab pot from a local fisherman, and when the tide was really low, he would walk down the beach and anchor the pot in the sand, then at the next low tide he would go down and see if we had caught anything. This was really exciting as there could be anything from a couple of Lady Crabs, a chancre, or once or twice even a lobster! We also collected winkles and limpets which when cooked were quite delicious, you would have to pull the winkles out of their shells with a pin, rather a slow procedure when you were really hungry. We would also gather Carrageen Moss {sea weed} and it would be washed many times to remove as much sand as possible, never all, but we did our best. Dad had made what looked like a coffee table but without a wooden top which was replaced by chicken wire. This stood in the garden and the moss was laid on it to dry and bake in the sun. My mother would then take it into the kitchen and work some miracle which I never investigated, and then it would appear on the dining table looking for all the world like white blanc-mange. The shock came when you tasted it, the texture was the same, but instead of the lovely sugary taste that one remembered there was a mouthful of something salty, but we soon got accustomed to that and looked forward to this treat every Sunday!

So the months passed and we did very well thank you, but as usual the Germans put a stop to this.

They mined all the beaches, and as if that was not enough deterrent to stop us going on the beaches, the put rolls of barbed wire all along the sea walls. No more food there!

I had many lovely patients on the female ward, but had one or two favorites. One in particular was very special and when the day arrived for her to go home I felt very sad. I helped her to get her things together for when her family came to fetch her. Last of all she reached into her locker and brought out a paper bag, handing it to me, she said;

"This is for your dinner as a thank you for the kindness you have shown me whilst I have been in here". We were giving each other a little hug when her brother arrived, and a few minutes later, she was gone.

I looked into the bag and in it was a Jerusalem artichoke. I had never seen one before let alone tasted one, but it was food, and I could not wait to get off duty to cook my delicious meal.

At just a little after two I left the hospital and almost ran across the meadow back to my 'digs'. No' one was at home but we had been given permission to use the kitchen if we wanted to, and I had never had reason to until now, but I couldn't wait. Not having seen an artichoke before I had no idea how to cook it, but at a guess I decided to treat it like a small cabbage. I washed it under the tap several times, and then popped it into a saucepan with water, and put it on to boil. I have to admit that while it was cooking the smell was nauseating, but I was very hungry and tried to ignore it.

After half an hour I took the pan off the gas and strained the water off into the sink. The odour was putrid, but it was food. I rolled the artichoke on to a plate and thought how nice it would be if I had a little salt, or even a spoonful of gravy, but there was nothing like that in the cupboard.

I stuck the fork into it and cut off a slice, I tried not to breathe as I lifted the fork to my mouth and took my first mouthful. Heavens! It was disgusting, but I was hungry and thought perhaps the second taste would not be quite so bad, but it was even worse! I was hungry enough to persevere and it was with great relief that I swallowed the last mouthful.

After washing up and putting away the dishes I had used I stumbled up the stairs to my bedroom. I was feeling so sick I could hardly reach the bed, but my afternoon off at my home was forgotten as I lay trying to ignore the terrible taste at the back of my throat. Several times I thought I would have to get up, but eventually I fell asleep and stayed that way until a faint glow filled my room and I realised that it was morning.

It was several weeks after this that a neighbour gave my mother half a loaf of German sour bread, and mum gave me a thick slice of it to take back to my digs. When I arrived on duty the next day I had my bread wrapped in paper in my uniform pocket. One of the nurses was making soup from stinging nettles in the duty room. She had made a huge saucepan full and invited any of the nurses to help themselves. I thought about it for a while, and when it was time for me to go down to the nurse's dining-room for lunch I decided to give it a try. I helped myself to a large soup plate full and carried it carefully down the stone steps. Seated at the table I unwrapped the bread from my pocket and breaking it into small pieces I dropped the sour bread into the nettle soup. Three spoonfuls later I laid the spoon back into the soup and made a dash for the toilet!!

The situation regarding food was so acute now, everyone was hungry, almost starving. The Islanders, the Germans and the Foreign workers, with the result that many of the Islanders pets were disappearing without trace and at last it dawned on us that the unpredictable was happening. These little animals were being used as food. The thought was horrific but was no fantasy.

My lovely cousin, Eileen, our fathers were brothers, had a beautiful dog named Sally, and she was locked in and outhouse in their garden at night for safety. Every morning my cousin would go out to unlock the door and let Sally free.

One morning as Eileen crossed the garden she thought the door looked slightly ajar. On closer inspection she discovered it was, and the lock had been forced. With a trembling heart, she pushed the door open and as she entered it was as she had expected, her precious pet was gone.

The family spent the entire morning searching the fields around their home. A German soldier billeted near by had made a habit of visiting them to try and make friends. He would show them photographs of his wife and family and say how he longed to go home. He came forward and helped them in their search for Sally, but it was all to no avail.

It was the next day after the sad loss of her dog that the same German who had helped them with their search walked in through their back door. He carried in his hand a small parcel wrapped in newspaper,

"For you" he said, handing it to Aunty Mim. She laid it on the kitchen table, and unwrapping it found a small joint of meat.

Her eyes shun with excitement at the thought of the scrumptious meal she would prepare that evening for her hungry family. Suddenly Eileen jumped to her feet.

"NO, she yelled, "Take it away, we don't want it".

"Eileen, whatever—".

"Oh mum!" she faced her mother with tears in her eyes, "Can't you see, it's my dog". And it probably was!!

****

Just when we had all come to the conclusion that we were going to starve to death a rumour ran riot that the Red Cross were going to send us food parcels. It was such a cruel rumour to spread and although deep in our hearts we knew it was impossible, we had just a very faint glimmer of hope that it could be true. Glory be! It was true.

We thought we would have one parcel per household, and waited impatiently to see if it would ever come true or if it was just another fairy tale to boost morale.

Then when we had almost given up hope, and were very near starvation, on December 24th. 1944 the news flashed like lightening through every parish in the Island that the magical ship the Vega had sailed into Guernsey waters loaded with Red Cross parcels of food for every Islander, also medical and surgical supplies-------and for those who cared, like my poor mother –cigarettes. Soon after cigarettes were no longer available she and a friend were having afternoon tea, and the subject went around to how much they missed a smoke with their mint tea.

"Can we not think of some sort of substitute for tobacco?" my mum enquired.

"Wish we could" came the reply.

"What about rose petals, if we dried them thoroughly, then rolled them in paper, what do you think" Deciding it was worth a try they gathered heaps of roses from the garden and pulling off the petals, put them on the window sill to dry in the sun.

Two days later the friend returned and they found the petals crisp and dry.

"I have brought some packing paper" and the two of them sat and cut little pieces of paper about the size of the old Rizla cigarette papers.

My mother produced an old cigarette maker and they stuffed masses of the petals into it. Next they put a piece of the paper into position, then closing the machine they rolled the cigarette and licking the edges, opened the machine and out came what looked like a perfect cigarette! With eager hands they quickly made another one, then together they each put one into their mouth and lighting a match got ready for their first inhalation for a long time. As the flame touched the edge of the paper it immediately consumed paper and petals and ran straight up to the tip burning their lips. With a yelp of pain they both spat the ash unto the floor, and after the initial shock resolved into fits of laughter.

But I digress: The Vega sailed in with its precious cargo but we had to wait several days for the announcement in the local Press telling us when and where to collect our boxes with their precious contents.

When ours arrived at our house, I was overjoyed to find that I was to have a box all to myself. With trembling hand I prised it open, and in it was a tin of Spam, tin of peaches [fruit at last], packet of biscuits, pat of butter, small jar of jam, a small Swiss roll, a bar of chocolate and a packet of Woodbine cigarettes, and so it was I started smoking, I did not want to, and I did not enjoy it, but they were in MY box and so they belonged to ME, and I wasn't sharing, and that was what put me on the slippery slope to becoming a smoker! However I conquered that habit later on, and have not smoked since.

Hunger is cruel, and in the beginning of 1945 the German soldiers were terribly emaciated, walking around like ghosts of their former selves, and bore all the signs of defeat. Remembering the days when they had sat at heavily laden tables while the Local people were eating cabbage leaves and potato peels, when they were lucky enough to get them, it was very difficult to feel any pity for them.

On Thursday 3rd of May 1945, the Vega made her fifth visit and brought with her;

22,940 parcels, 224 bales of clothing, 173 bales of footwear, 133 sacks of sugar, 55 sacks of salt,185 tons of flour, 14 cases of yeast, and 37 cases of soap.

I remember vividly the first white loaf that arrived at our house. It was so white and spongy, and after my mother had sliced it ready for our special tea, she began to put butter from our Red Cross parcels on the slices, and I helpfully stopped her saying;

"You don't put butter on cake, Mum".

"This isn't cake, darling, it is bread" she informed me. I could not believe it, was this really what we could expect to eat EVERY DAY? What heaven, what bliss!!

****

Gwen and I had been given a crystal set each together with ear-phones from friends in the underground, and we had them very safely hidden in our bedroom, and when we needed material for a Lyric show, we would lock ourselves into our bedroom, then Gwen would take down the music, and I would take down the words, we would practise it for a few days and then perform it in our show.

One late afternoon for the want of something better to do we decided to go to our room and listen to see if we could find any new material to use. Getting our sets from beneath the floor boards where they were hidden, we settled down, Gwen on her bed and me lying on my tummy on the floor between the two beds each with our ear-phones on, we twiddled the cats whisker until we heard the BBC. Then came the strains of a tune we had heard a few times before, I looked up at Gwen and she was looking at me. Raising her eyebrows and lifting her shoulders in a questioning gesture, I nodded my head in the affirmative and we both began to write.

There came a break in the singing, so I lifted my head to look at my sister. I was amazed to see she had removed her ear-phones and was staring at the door with a look of terror on her face.

I lay my face on the carpet and looked towards the door, and there, as I feared, was a pair of jackboots beside the half open door. In our eagerness to listen in to the radios we had forgotten to lock the door. This was the first and only time that we had ever done this and as fate would have it a German tried the door.

I raised myself up so that my face was just above the bed and I saw that it was George who had a room across the landing from ours.

"So this is what you do in your room" he sneered in broken English "You know you can be shot for this".

Oh we knew all right!

"So, what must we do now?"

Complete silence from us, we were too scared to speak anyway.

"I do not like to be the one to report you to the Commandant, but you have disobeyed orders made by the German Forces, and you must both pay".

More silence, then Gwen said in a timid voice, "You can have our radios if you want them".

"Why would I want such rubbish, I have a lovely radio of my own."

"Oh you're not going to report us are you, please don't."

He was silent for a few seconds, and then he said;

"I tell you what; I will do a deal with you. The next time that ship comes with parcels for you both you will give your parcels to me, and you will do that every time you get a parcel, and that way I will not report you.

As there was complete silence he waited a moment, then;

"Is it a deal?"

I was too shocked to answer, and then I heard Gwen say in almost a whisper, "Yes, it is a deal".

George went out and shut the door.

I rolled over the bed and dropping to the floor reached up and locked the door.

We rolled back the corner of the carpet and removing the loose board in the floor we put away our crystal sets without so much as a word.

As I lay in bed that night I was fighting to hold back the tears, never more to have my own Red Cross parcel, no more lovely things to eat, back to the days of dreadful hunger pains, and all because I had been stupid enough not to lock the bedroom door. I hardly slept that night, and neither did my sister, I knew that because I could hear her twisting and turning, and once or twice I fancied I heard a sob.

I was unhappy enough to hope that the food he would steal from me would choke him!

Chapter 10.

Every morning I would open my bedroom door and peer carefully out to make sure George was nowhere in sight, and then would gallop down the stairs to the kitchen for breakfast.

Mother soon became aware that there was something amiss with her girls, and hoped it would pass, but when it carried on for several days she could resist no longer, and one morning she sat down to breakfast with us and tackled us both.

"O.K. girls, let's have it, what is wrong with you both, have you had a row of some sort or what is the matter, you don't seem as full of fun as usual come on, let's have it, what is the trouble?"

At first neither of us wanted to tell her the truth, we were both so ashamed of the fact that we had forgotten to lock the door and had put the whole family in danger by our stupidity.

"Come on". She coaxed "Who is going to speak first, I'm waiting".

We shifted uncomfortably on our chairs, I waited for Gwen to say something, but she was waiting for me to speak first. I suddenly felt I needed to have Mum on my side; maybe she would help me out of my dilemma as she had always done whenever I had had problems at school, but they all seemed so insignificant compared with this new situation.

"I am going to tell mum everything I blurted out to Gwen" and she just glared at me as if to say "What a fool" Mum did not speak; I think she was afraid to silence me. Slowly I began to tell her about what had happened in our bedroom and as a result Gwen and I would never have a Red Cross parcel again, and how we would have to starve again like before.

 Mum listened in silence until I finished speaking, I glanced at her, and she seemed to be smiling.

"Which German was it?" was all she said. I was dumbfounded, what difference could it make which German it was, our problem was we would never again receive a food parcel, how could it possibly matter which German it was?

Gwen could see I was becoming angry so she decided to help me out.

"It was the one called George staying in room no. 5, he was really angry and said he would only not report us to the Commandant if we would both give him our Red Cross parcels from now on".

"Is that all he said" my mother asked with a most mystical smile on her face.

"Yes it was, what else would you expect him to say, that he would shoot us after we had given them to him?" I was really angry by then, my mother was really making light of the whole affair. She didn't seem to realize how frightened we both were.

"Mum, help us, what can we do, we need your help so badly please don't tease us about it". Came from Gwen.

"I am not the one doing the teasing,"

"What do you mean". We asked, both nearly in tears.

"I think it was George teasing, not me, he left Guernsey two days ago, he has been sent to the Russian Front, I am afraid he wont be back to collect your food parcels, he came to say goodbye and asked me to tell you to remember to lock your bedroom door in future"!!!

One of the many days that stand out in my memory was my seventeenth birthday. We had long stopped celebrating birthdays because of the lack of food and the impossibility of obtaining presents, but my mother had managed to get a beautiful lace tablecloth in exchange for several of my sister's and my school blouses which no longer fitted us and taking it to a dressmaker had secretly had her make me a dress. She gave it to me on the morning of my birthday and I was overwhelmed, it was so beautiful, and to make it even more wonderful, it fitted like a glove. Although we were going to be just the family I decided to wear it that night.

The day went really well, several friends called to wish me a happy birthday, and although no presents were exchanged we had a lovely afternoon. Gwen and I played on the pianos and we all sang and danced the afternoon away. Everyone was thoughtful enough to leave quite early as was the norm in those days because we knew a meal was out of the question.

Any way Mum explained when we were alone that we would be eating later than usual so did I want to go upstairs and get my new dress on, and then she added that there was going to be a very little surprise for me so not to come down till I was called. This was very intriguing and so I took all my time getting dressed and seeing to my hair and face.

There seemed to be a lot of movement coming from below but I decided not to investigate and wait to be called. My dress looked even prettier in the electric light and I twisted and twirled in front of the mirror and came to the realization that at last I had grown up. Lovely thought.

Eventually, just when I was beginning to get really browned off with the delay, I heard Gwen coming up the stairs and entering the room said they were ready for me.

"Outside" she ordered as we reached the back door. I just stared at her in amazement; "Outside?" I queried.

"Uh huh" came the reply as she opened the back door.

To our right was a sort of ramp which led to a double chalet which was all in darkness, I went first and on opening the door felt for the light switch. As the room flooded with light;

"Surprise, surprise" came the cry, and there to my amazement were almost every member of the Lyric No. 1 Company, and as if that was not enough a large table was in the centre of the room and it held FOOD, very small amounts of everything, but so many different things it was obvious that every guest had made some sort of contribution.

There was lots of kissing and hugging and "Happy birthday to you" being sung, and at last we all sat down, that was when the door opened and in walked my mother carrying a birthday cake topped with 17 candles. My boyfriend being in the trade had made it and covered it with pink fondant. Goodness only knows where he got the ingredients from, but that was a question no one ever asked during the occupation.

I rose from my chair and as I leaned forward to blow out the candles, the tenor from our company stood up and in his silvery voice sang:- "I saw you in the light of seventeen candles, So much like a rose beginning to bloom-----" As he finished and the candles were extinguished everybody clapped, and then we set about tucking into our gorgeous, almost pre-war feast.

When we had eventually finished, if a whole flock of vultures had been let loose in that room the table would not have been barer. The only thing missing had been something tasty to drink, all we had was tap water, but nobody thought about that at the time, and feeling more than satisfied we moved back into the hotel and the party started in earnest.

Gwen and I took it in turns to play the piano and we sang the night away.

Now and again for a little break we would play gramophone records and dance with each other, and of course all the members of the company took a turn to entertain, and I am quite confident there has never been a party quite like it before or since.

Then another surprise, my father brought in a bottle of Calvados, again no questions asked, but then the party really went off with a swing.

We sang, we danced, we laughed, and for a while completely forgot that the rest of the hotel was full of the German enemy and what we found most surprising thinking about it later, was the fact that not one of them tried to gate crash, amazing!

It must have been nearly half past four in the morning before we slowly began to give up, and bit by bit every armchair, every settee, and even spaces on the floor were occupied by a very sleepy person who had to wait anyway for the curfew to lift before they could make their way home.

So my seventeenth birthday ended, and I was happier that night than I had been for over four years, and I, for the first time in all those years began to get a glimmer of hope that maybe we would after all come out of the horror and find sunshine on the other side.

****

The closeness of people in those days was something never known before or since, if anyone was in trouble, especially if it concerned the German forces, every other person, (almost without exception) would rally round and offer to help.

One very clear indication of this was when we had notice that we were to be sent to a concentration camp in Germany and before Sister Young had helped us out.

Two young brothers, known to us only by sight, called one evening and asked if they could have a word with my parents. They were invited in and Gwen and I made ourselves scarce.

The elder of the two spoke first.

"I understand that you and Mrs. Smith have had orders to leave the Island and to take your two daughters with you?"

"That's right" answered Dad.

"Well at this terrible time my brother and I wondered if we could help".

"In what way?" from Dad.

The younger brother of the two then spoke up.

"My brother and I are both single, our parents evacuated, we live alone, and if it would take a weight off your shoulders, we are willing to marry your girls and so avoid them having to go with you.

This was followed by dead silence until at last my mother spoke.

"What a marvelous gesture you have both just made."

"With a strict understanding that it would be a marriage of convenience and a divorce would be granted as soon as the war is over if either or both of the girls so desired", came from the older brother.

As neither of the men seemed to want to leave, the discussion went on at length.

Eventually my mother took hold of the reins.

"You are two of the nicest boys I know, and I would be very proud to have either of you as a son-in-law, but when the evacuation took place we knew we would either all go together or stay together, and as a similar situation has arisen, I think my husband will agree with me that we will again all stick together as a family once again".

It was such a lovely sacrifice they were willing to make, and it must have taken a considerable amount of discussing before they decided to call, having finally decided to put forward the offer they seemed reluctant to take no for an answer.

Finally they realized their very kind offer was being rejected and after shaking hands all round and being thanked once again, they finally allowed my father to see them to the door.

"If you should change your mind just give us a call", was their parting remark.

When our parents told us what they had called to say, we were very flattered, and a little disappointed to hear our parents had refused their offer!

Later in our bedroom we discussed the issue, we decided they were quite good looking.

"Which one would you have chosen?" My sister asked me.

"Which one would have wanted me,? We will never know" and we both fell about laughing.

Chapter 11.

When we performed our very last Christmas show at the Lyric we had no idea it would be the last. How could we know that our liberation from the occupation was just five months away? And in our ignorance we put on not only a super show to try to cheer up all the downhearted, but also a brave face to pretend we did not care anyway!

We rehearsed all month and put everything we had into it. Lots of cheerful carols were included, and all the dances and various scenes had a truly Christmas flavor.

Finding costumes, especially for us dancers was a nightmare, but in all the five years that we performed we always managed to come up with something new, we either begged, borrowed, but never stole, from neighbours, relatives and friends who I must say were always more than willing to help if they could. I think they used to sit in the audience and when we came on stage would whisper to the person next to them, things like;

"You see that skirt she is wearing, that is one of my old dining-room curtains!"

But did we care? Not likely.

When the Christmas show was planned I was frantic about what I would wear for my solos.

Then out of the blue, a lady arrived at our front door carrying a large bag.

"I wonder, "she enquired "if you would be interested in exchanging something from your Red Cross parcel for this?"

I invited her in and in the kitchen she unfolded her parcel to reveal the most beautiful apricot coloured taffeta evening dress that flounced out to the ground in marvelous folds, it was like something out of a fairy story. I was completely overwhelmed.

"What would you want in exchange" I was almost afraid to ask. I was sure it was going to be way out of my depths.

"Well you see it belonged to my sister who evacuated, she is a little older than me, and I know you will agree that I am now past this sort of gown, and I know she would be pleased to think it had gone towards getting me a little food".

I ran upstairs and brought down my Red Cross parcel which I had only recently received and opening it up asked her what she would like to choose.

Taking out a box of butter asked;

"Can you spare this"?

I took out a small jar of paste, a bar of chocolate, and 10 Woodbine cigarettes and went to give them to her.

"Oh no, not all that ", she gasped.

"Yes indeed" I argued "I am so delighted with the frock".

She argued no further and left quite happily with her cache of goodies, and I stormed upstairs to try on my beautiful dress. It could not have fitted better if I had had it made to my measurements. My family was overjoyed too and could not believe that a stranger had just turned up at the door with it. They all agreed that I must have been born under a lucky star, and I knew they were right.

This was to be the very last Christmas show we would ever put on, but of course we did not know that at the time. How, after five long years could we imagine that liberation was so close?

We had after three weeks of tiring rehearsals already staged one show for the German censors.

These consisted of sometimes two and sometimes three Officers who would sit in the front row smoking large cigars, a vacant look on their faces which never wavered; they did not laugh at our comedians jokes, nor clap for any of the items.

When the show was over, our producer would meet them and they would either say

"All is good, carry on".

Or they might ask a question about one or the other of the jokes if they thought it might have a hidden meaning concerning the German Reich.

Anyway, in this instance they gave us the all clear to carry on.

We had performed many shows over the years, many times using the same title but always with new ingredients, such shows as:

"Anchors Aweigh".

"The Old Bull and Bush".

"Café Continental".

"Ye Old Tyme Music Hall" and many more too numerous to mention.

Now we were ready to perform the show of the year. A lot of practice had gone into it and we wanted the audience to go away feeling we had given of our all.

At each corner at the front of the stage, our carpenter had erected a slope leading down to the auditorium with a hand rail on each side, and so our first performance of the week began.

It was hilarious with loads of audience participation, and the whole show went with a lovely swing.

Encores were asked for but could not be given as it was necessary to keep to strict time so that the audience and players could get home before curfew.

At last the show was over and we all walked forward to take our final curtain, but instead of bowing in the usual way, the two members on each end of the line walked a way down the slope and encouraging the front row to come forward, took their hands, and crossing our arms in the traditional way we all held hands.

That was the cue for our conductor to begin the music and we all sang "Auld Lang Syne" with such gusto that we almost raised the roof, and although the Germans in the audience did not know the words, they linked arms like the rest of us, and just nodded and smiled in time to the music.

Who was the enemy, and who was the friend? It was very hard to tell at a time like that. Music has a mysterious way of joining items, but they all fell apart again when the music stopped.

Still our producer stepped forward and said;

"Merry Christmas to all, and to all a Good Night", and I am sure the ovation and cheers must have echoed halfway down to the Town.

To this day, I accuse Hitler of robbing me my teenage years. These most important years when a person is changing from a child to an adult mean so very much and are usually punctuated by a close family unit, making voyages abroad to broaden the mind, and reaching across the world to enhance and strengthen ones whole attitude towards life. We teenagers were deprived of all that.

Instead we existed through these years on a tiny Island, slowly but surely growing out of our clothes and only second hand pieces or old curtains made into frocks and skirts to replace them. No good dreaming about high heeled satin shoes to replace school shoes, fast becoming too small, only clog like shoes with wooden soles sent over from France in the later years, causing us to overbalance and injure our ankles. Then there was the matter of nourishing food needed for growing children. The amounts grew less and less, and became so sparse, that things such as bananas, chocolate, oranges, ice-cream and so many lovely things became a faint memory to us older children, and unknown to the younger ones.

We would dream of sitting by a roaring fire, eating a bag of crisps whilst listening to some dreamy music playing on our radio, we would dream all this whilst sitting in front of an empty grate. Drinking water from the tap in dead silence.

We could not understand why we had been forgotten by the Mother Land, we felt like children waking from the middle of an horrific dream, sitting up in bed, crying and screaming for our mother to come in and hold us close telling us all would be well. ------but no mother came!

Had we been forgotten? Oddly enough, just two days after the liberation the following announcement appeared in the Guernsey Evening Press:-

'If the Germans had not surrendered, all plans were ready for an invasion of the Channel Islands by British Forces to 'get rid of the blackguards'. These plans had been ready for a year. The British Authorities had known pretty well all the time what the Germans were doing in Guernsey, and their intelligence reports had kept them well up to date regarding the strength of the fortifications and the resistance they were likely to encounter when a landing was made'.

Then when all hope of survival was fading fast, it was a few minutes after 6 o'clock evening, May 6th.1945, that the news flashed around the Island that Peace was imminent. Those of us who still had radios hidden heard that the Prime Minister was expected very soon to broadcast the news for which the whole world was waiting, after which His Majesty the King would speak to his subjects.

Throughout Monday the tension in Guernsey was unbelievable, then again in the evening on the 6 o'clock news came the glorious announcement that Germany had signed her capitulation to the three Powers at nineteen minutes to three o'clock on Monday morning.

We all listened with great interest to the speech made by Mr. Winston Churchill on Tuesday May 8th when he said that hostilities would end officially at one minute after midnight that night. Then went on to say

"In the interest of saving lives, the Cease Fire began yesterday to be sounded all along the fronts, and our dear Channel Islands are also to be freed today."

So maybe he was the 'mum' who came to console us after our nightmare??

Liberation
Poem wrote circa 1945

It's over, God, it's over, I can't believe it's true;

It's the first time I've seen my father cry,

For no matter how much trouble, or how short of food we were,

There was always hope and laughter in his eye.

It's over, yes it's over, our siege is really through,

Liberation forces landed here at noon,

I don't know when I'm going to see those super English troops;

But no matter when, it just can't be too soon!

It's over, God it's over, we're laughing through our tears,

The hunger and the heartbreak all are past;

And everybody's hugging everybody else today,

And our Scottish flag is flying at the mast.

It's over, God, it's over, what better time than this

To be alone for just a sec' or two,

To clasp my hands together, to gently close my eyes

And thank the One who brought us safely through.

Chapter 12.

So at last it was really here. The day that the 23,000 Islanders had longed for but had begun to fear would never materialize actually dawned on May 9th. 1945. The sun rose slowly over Herm Island and spread its gentle but glowing rays gently across the Island of Guernsey, but the glow was not nearly as strong as that which was held in every Islander's heart. The atmosphere was aglow with the electricity of expectation as we waited during a very long morning for three o'clock to arrive.

I spent the latter part of that morning in the garden with my father getting our flag out of its wrappings and tied up ready for the big moment when we would send it up to the top of our flagpole in honour of the great occasion.

While we were kneeling on the grass one of the Germans living in our home came through the gate and walked over to us and asked what we were doing. My father told him and he said,

"No, Tetti, this you must not do, there is not going to be a liberation. I have just come from the Regal Cinema, we have had a very big meeting, and we have been ordered by Admiral Hueffmeier to fight to keep this Island, we will fight to the last blade of grass".

I stared at my father with a look of great disappointment on my face and was surprised to see him smiling.

"Don't worry too much about your last big stand, at three o'clock this afternoon this flag is going to be hoisted to the top of our flagpole and will fly out in the wind for all to see that at last we have been liberated. Just awhile before you were sitting in the Regal Cinema this morning Major-General Heine of the Luftwaffe signed the surrender terms," and my father was smiling even more.

The German turned on his Jackboot heel and marched back into the house.

Worried after so many years of obeying orders, I looked my father in the eyes.

"Are you absolutely sure Dad, please don't take any risks at this late stage".

My father gave me a lovely wink. "I'm sure" he said.

A little while later my mother and Gwen came to join us.

It was then I noticed how the streets were becoming crowded, and several people were wandering into our garden.

"It is just coming up to three" said one of them, "just one minute to go"

We all stood very close to each other and then at that moment it happened. A church bell rang out, followed by another and yet another until every church bell in the Island was ringing out its cheerful message, we were FREE!!!

Up shot our flag to the top of the flagpole and we all began to sing 'God Save the King', quickly followed by 'Rule Britannia' and of course we rounded that off with Guernsey's own 'Sarnia Cherie.

Then the tears began to flow, everyone was kissing everybody else, people were shaking hands with each other, there was hugging and back slapping and just general jollification.

My parents were holding each other close and I heard my father say to my mother;

"It's all over, darling, we can begin to live again at last".

The afternoon went all too quickly, but the evening was a never to be forgotten occasion.

A friend of the family who was a farmer from St. Andrews, came down to Cobo in his tractor attached to which was a very large size scoop on wheels, and it was into this scoop that many of us climbed and then away we went up to Saumarez Park where a liberation dance was being celebrated in the side hall.

We rattled up the hill called Les Pins, singing at the tops of our voices, no fear anymore of being stopped by patrols or overtaken by a car full of German officers just waiting to see us in jail; we were FREE in every sense of the word.

How we danced that night, wooden soles or no wooden soles. My feet were sore and bleeding by the end of the party, but did I care? Can a duck swim?

Around nine o'clock in the evening everyone became a little bit fidgety, as the usual time for curfew came around, but then the realization dawned on us all that we could stay out as long as we chose and no one would stop us on the way home—Bliss!

****

So the inhabitants of the Island had been separated in half by the evacuation. Who is to say which half were right?

Those is in the Motherland had to endure sleepless nights in bomb shelters only to come out in the morning perhaps to find their home in ruins.

Had we all remained in Guernsey we would most definitely have starved well before hostilities ceased. So let us not determine who were right and who were wrong, the evacuees, or the stay-at-homes.

And so our long ordeal is over. No more will we hear the tramp, tramp, tramp of the jackboots on our streets, never again see the green grey uniforms meeting us as we turn each corner, gone are the foreign words echoing on the breeze, and gone the fear lingering in our hearts of what the next calamity is going to be.

To be able to talk freely without the fear that perhaps the person you are talking to is in cahoots with the 'Jerrys'.

So now all that is fading into the gloom, but the memory of the years from July 1st 1940 to May 9th. 1945 will remain with those who endured it for ever more.

THE END

OR MAYBE THE BEGINNING?

6978325R00084

Printed in Great Britain
by Amazon.co.uk, Ltd.,
Marston Gate.